MY MAMA MARIE

Joan Errea

Center for Basque Studies

My Mama Marie

Joan Errea

Center for Basque Studies
University of Nevada, Reno

The book was published with generous financial support from the Basque government

Center for Basque Studies
University of Nevada, Reno
Reno, Nevada

Unless otherwise specified, photographs courtesy of the author, Alice Norcutt, and Daniel Montero
Illustrations by Bert Paris

Design by Kimberly Daggett

Cover: Photo of Pleasant Valley Paris Ranch and portrait of Marie

Library of Congress Cataloging-in-Publication Data
Errea, Joan.
My mama Marie / Joan Errea.
pages cm
Summary: "The history of the author's mother from her youth in the Basque Country, her immigration to the United States, and her ranching life in the American West"-- Provided by publisher.
ISBN 978-1-935709-39-8 (pbk.)
1. Etcheverry, Marie Jeanne, 1911-1981. 2. Basque American women--West (U.S.)--Biography. 3. Basque Americans--West (U.S.)--Biography. 4. Mothers and daughters--United States. 5. Errea, Joan--Family. I. Title.

CT275.E735E77 2013
978'.033092--dc23
[B]

2013021564

To my grandson, Martin J. Iroz. He is the light of my life and fills my world with love. He makes my heart dance! He is one of the reasons that I wrote this book.

Love always,
Amatchi

Marie Jeanne Paris Etcheverry

Alice Paris Norcutt and Marie Jeanne Paris Etcheverry

CONTENTS

ACKNOWLEDGMENTS

This book has been illustrated by Bert Paris of Battle Mountain, Nevada. Bert is the son of the author's brother Arnaud, who has been the guiding influence in my life, and the greatest encouragement in my "abilities or disabilities."

Soldier Creek Basin, Ruby Mountains

Introduction

FOLLOWING MARIE

My *Mama Marie* is a remarkable story. On the surface it is a fairly simple story written by a grandmother for her grandson about her own mother. However, I believe even more so it is the story of two girls who became two women, and two men who in very different ways influenced to a great degree the girls' development, and the women's personalities. The first girl, Marie, was raised under trying – to say the least – circumstances in the Northern (French) Basque Country town of Banca (Banka in Batua Basque). Her father, a French army resister, had fled across the border to Spain to escape service and her mother took refuge with her relative, an abusive priest – the first important male figure of the story, and the villain of Marie's childhood – who treated the family as his personal slaves and who indentured the young girl to a cruel mistress. After many adventures, this girl then braved the passage to the United States, traveled alone across the breadth of the country, and arrived at a desolate little train stop in Currie, Nevada. A place she had certainly never heard of. To her, it must have seemed that she had arrived at the end of the earth.

The familiar sound of Basque was the only thing that she could understand about this new land, but it did not come from anyone she knew, it came from a young stranger, a young man – the second man of the story, the man who would become her beloved husband and the author's beloved Aita – who dared to poke fun at her predicament and helped her settle into her new land and unsettle her in a way no one in the Old Country had ever done.

The rest was history, as they say, but history in the complicated way of immigrants fighting to create a life in a landscape that was in many ways inhospitable: Marie worked at the hotel in Currie, then in the Basque-owned hotel in Eureka, Nevada, where she rekindled her relationship with the young man who had first spoken to her in Basque and who had infuriated and intrigued her. Their romance followed the rhythm of their homeland: at dances playing the Old Country's music and following the Old Country's steps, but their life together was distinctly American. After their marriage, they moved to a lonely line cabin in the Secret Pass of the Ruby

Mountains in Elko County, Nevada, and the girl, now woman, Marie, bore three children in line cabins and sheep wagons following her hard-working husband and their inevitable bands of sheep. They saved enough to buy a ranch called Forest Home in the White River Valley, some eighty miles south of Lund, Nevada, then enough to buy another ranch in Pleasant Valley, south of Winnemucca, Nevada.

It was first in sheep camps and then at Forest Home that the second girl, the author, Joan Errea, came into her own. A self-described Basque-speaking tomboy, her relationship with her mother forms the emotional heart of this book. It was a complicated and in many ways difficult relationship. A relationship bound by iron wills: on the one hand, a woman raised in difficult circumstances and with the strong influence of an abusive figure; on the other, a strong-willed little girl who did not want to conform to the roles that were expected of her. Behind their test of wills, the men, one a shadowy and dark figure, the other shining and light. Though the story is often funny, this tension, this battle of wills infuses the book with a depth that goes much deeper. In some ways, I believe, it serves as a metaphor for the process of immigration and assimilation, of leaving behind the old and embracing the new, all the while holding on dearly to the traditions, language, and ways of life of the Old Country.

It was this tension that first intrigued the editorial board at the Center and made this book stand out. As we worked through the manuscript, I found myself more and more intrigued by the story, and, by extension, the places where this story played out. So, one weekend as we finished up the book's editing process, I decided to retrace, as much as I could, the steps of *My Mama Marie*. The story had grabbed me, and I wanted to experience firsthand the places where it had taken place. So I drove east from Reno on Highway 50, the "Loneliest Road in America."

My first stop was Eureka; there I wandered about and asked locals which building had been the Basque hotel, the Eureka Hotel. One woman couldn't remember. The young girl at the museum had no idea. Then, standing alongside Highway 50 (which serves as Eureka's main street), an old man in a battered cowboy hat drove up in a beaten up truck. I asked if he was from the town. He said no, "out in the Valley." I asked if he remembered a Basque hotel: he said yes, that one, pointing across the street to a decaying stone building. In the 1930s, he said, it was owned by Basques. Now the stone building has a faded sign that reads EUREKA HOTEL. A closed Chinese restaurant takes up the ground floor. The rest remaines abandoned. The old man told me it had been run by the Goyhenetche's. I left the man to his business and walked across Highway 50 to stand in front of its closed doors and tried to imagine it spilling out young sheepherders, the loud sound of accordion music playing inside and the more muffled steps of the dancers while young men, mostly, and a few girls took air in the front, on the Main Street, speaking Basque to each other. I imagined young Marie, stepping onto the dance floor and catching the eye, and the heart, of Arnaud Paris.

I drove farther east, deeper into Marie's history, to Currie. Now part of a ranch, I arrived in the late afternoon. The tracks remain, overgrown with desert weeds, the old depot, its windows broken and boarded up with plywood, and the two-story hotel, still retaining something grand despite its advanced decay. The ranch yard was jumbled with pickups – both working and not – horse trailers, and the other implements of a working ranch. There were dogs and horses, a very friendly pony, but no people to ask permission to wander the area, so I did anyway, first circling the old boarded up hotel and then walking along the tracks to the depot. In my mind, I cleared away the ranch, removed the weeds from the tracks and in their place put a smoking locomotive, and a young girl stepping out, shielding her eyes against the glare and fearing that, after the green and lush Basque Country, she had stepped straight into the Inferno. Where the horse trailers were, I placed the team of horses handled by a young Basque man who, interested in the train's arrival (surely a big event in the little stop's day) put down his work and watched a pretty young girl disembark, and who then spoke to her in their shared tongue. A language spoken by very few in the world and jealously guarded and defended.

As I was finishing up another pickup arrived with a young couple, ranch workers obviously, and I explained to them my interest in the place, but in reality I was imagining them as young Marie and Arnaud, working to create a life in a place most Americans imagine is nothing but history.

I continued on, deeper into the story, driving north along the eastern edge of the Ruby Mountains and crossing Secret Pass at sunset. The modern ranches have fenced in the open range, and I could find no sign of the line cabin where Marie and Arnaud had begun their life together, but the landscape has changed little: green rolling hills (in the early summer at least) leading into imposing mountains. A landscape that should, or could have daunted them, beaten them, as it did many others, but where they instead found opportunity. It was in these hills, or hills like them, where young Joan took her first steps, where Queenie the Australian shepherd served as babysitter and caregiver and Auncha the goat served as playmate and friend.

That night I camped at the mouth of Soldier

Creek, where the Paris sheep bands had had their summer range, which Joan writes about as the place where she spent her happiest days fishing with her father. In the morning I hiked up the steep creek canyon and then, where it opened up into a basin ringed with high mountains, I imagined the bands of sheep and the father and daughter walking, he with a gunnysack of the day's catch slung over his shoulder and she following along in the protective glow of her adored father.

I returned to my camp late in the afternoon after wandering along the creek and among the ponds and lakes of the Soldier Creek Basin, following in the footsteps, I imagined at least, of young Joan and Aita, watching the big bands of summer fat sheep dotting the hillside and seeing the white tents of wagons of the big summer camp. The sun was setting and I walked through the shadows from Soldier Mountain and the high country of the Rubies before emerging again into the bright Nevada light. Walking through shadow and light, I thought of how each of the places I had visited had shed a distinct light on the story, making me realize how very special it is. How much struggle had gone into creating a life, and how much was both gained and lost by it. *My Mama Marie* has the ring of this, of the truth of these places, and the truth of real stories: stories not dressed up with the trapping of myth, but the real stories of people, hard-working people, who instead of seeing only despair and abandonment, chose to forge ahead and to create a life, and in the process to leave their mark on the land. They are, for me, the true testaments of this book, and the reason why it stands out in the memory.

– Daniel Montero
Reno, Nevada, June 2013

The Currie Hotel, Currie, Nevada

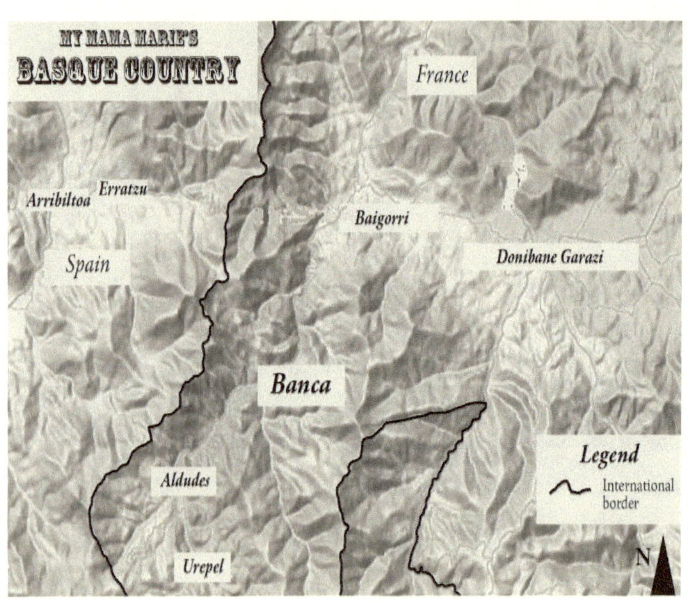
MY MAMA MARIE'S
BASQUE COUNTRY
France
Arribiltoa
Erratzu
Baigorri
Spain
Donibane Garazi
Banca
Aldudes
Urepel
Legend
International border
N

Winnemucca
Elko
Secret Pass
Soldier Cr.
Pleasant Valley
Ruby Mts.
Currie
Nevada
Reno
Eureka
Ely
Carson City
Lund
White River Valley
Las Vegas
MY MAMA
MARIE'S
NEVADA
N

Dear Mama,

I wrote this book to tell our family our story and the history of your life in Europe and in America.

I think that I was never able to tell you how greatly I loved you and how much I wish that you had been able to tell me what I always wanted so desperately to hear. I also believe – now that I have written this story – that you showed me in so many other ways and the million things you did for me. But, dear mama, what a great difference those three little words would have made in our lives! Always there but always unspoken.

You are always in my heart interlaced with the memory of Aita.

We both loved him so much, and he was the willing giver of so much love.

For our family, mama, I bare my heart to you to tell you now, I love you mama!

Marie Jeanne and Arnaud Paris, at their wedding

A slap on the innocent face,
to conquer a child,
Never tamed her soul
nor made her meek and mild.
She met the threats and pompous ways
with proud disdain.
Her flashing eyes and rebellious heart
masked hidden pain,
He appeared a saintly, holy man
but inside was a raging beast
What a tormented man he must have been,
My mama's uncle, the priest.
She thwarted him every chance she got,
disdaining free and wild
He failed in any conceivable way
to conquer the wayward child.

"He, who should have been so proud and tolerant of his acquired family, only appeared so in the public eye."

THE PRIEST

My mother, Marie Jeanne Goyhenetche, was born to Santiago Goyhenetche and Michaela Bayonnez Goyhenetche in 1911 in the French Pyrenees town of Banca (Banka in Batua Basque) in the Basque Country.

Her home was considered "fatherless" because her father, Santiago, had been forced into living in exile in Spain by the French government for refusing to serve in the army. He had been branded a *desertora*, or deserter, to his country. His life with his family was limited to a few clandestine visits with them when he could manage to sneak over the border to the French side. Those few visits were hurried and tearful to all the family despite the small gifts and food he could smuggle over to them.

His salary was given over to the uncle, a priest, who had acquired something like a power of attorney over his brother's home and family and financial affairs.

My grandfather's first wife had died at a young age, leaving him three sons to raise. By the time he met and married Michaela Bayonnez, those sons were grown and had moved to South America to become cattle ranchers. Marie Jeanne never knew her three older brothers except for the occasional gifts that they sent to the family. The money they sent was never seen by any of the children; it went straight to the greedy priest's coffers. Santiago, of course, was never aware of the situation and Grandmama, who was by nature a very shy, retiring person, was too cowed by Don Cruz, as the priest was known, for she never questioned his control over their finances.

Don Cruz was the reverend monsignor of the Catholic Church in Banca. He was a revered and respected man of the cloth in the deeply religious town, but was in reality a hypocrite and an abusive, self-centered, greedy man. He abused his power and dominated his brother's home and family with a heavy hand.

His sermons and his fiery temper kept the people in Banca in awe of him, and none dared to contradict him or question his teachings. All the children of the parish were petrified of him, as were the children of Grandfather and Grandmama Goyhenetche.

Marie Jeanne grew up in this strict abusive atmosphere, never being allowed to show her feelings or her emotions. Don Cruz was a total and dominant authority. She was a beautiful child with snappy black eyes that often sparkled with mischief, and she had a headful of rippling black hair that hung to her waist. She was sturdy and strong and always a willing worker. She had a fine personality when out of sight of Don Cruz, or "Aita Haundia," the "big father."

He, who should have been so proud and tolerant of his acquired family, only appeared so in the public eye. Most of the children were submissive, except the one with unquenchable fire in her eyes; she continued to defy him at every turn and met his often abusive intolerance with dry-eyed contempt. None threatened his authority more than wild Marie Jeanne, who was, in his eyes, condemned to the fires of Hell.

It was then the custom in Basque homes for the head of the house to tap his utensils against his glass to signal that he needs something or that he requires service at the table, so it was Marie Jeanne's duty to answer the tapping of the spoon on the glass at once.

One day Don Cruz, requiring a second helping of soup, tapped his glass and when Marie Jeanne was not fast enough to answer his summons, he gave her a cuff. She took the plate into the kitchen filled it with soup and spit in it a few times, and gleefully placed it in front of the man. Then she hid behind the door with

Banca. Photo courtesy of Catherine Çaldumbide.

her brother Louis giggling as they watched him consume the soup, spit and all. Of course, Louis was not one to discourage his little sister. Never mind that they waited all day for a lightning bolt to come out of the sky and strike Don Cruz, but when nothing happened, they became more brave and daring.

It was the custom for the father to eat first and then the family would sit down for their meal. Don Cruz weighed over three hundred pounds and I'm sure the pickings were sometimes meager when the family finally sat down. The priest had a large appetite and ate many strange and exotic things that Marie Jeanne and Louis figured were good for such a large man. Grandmama, on the other hand, would sometimes do without if one of the little ones needed more. She never lifted a finger to stop the abuse. She and her little ones were dependent on the father for their home, she could not risk offending him and instead suffered in silence. Santiago, trapped across the border due to his rejection of military service, never learned of this suffering. Even though the whole family often bore bruises, no one in the town would lift a finger. Santiago's visits were always arranged through his brother's hands, so he took care to arrange them when none of the bruises showed. Since Don Cruz greased palms and gave some blessings to the authorities in order to arrange a visit now and again between bruises, I don't believe Grandfather was ever aware of any trouble. I am surprised that the children never told. Perhaps it was fear that kept them from it.

At very early ages all the children were farmed out to friends in neighboring towns and the few francs they earned were paid to Don Cruz for the family coffers.

One by one, the boys slipped out of the clutches of the monsignor. Marie Jeanne, however, was sent as a maid to an elderly lady who was a very "dear" friend of the malevolent priest. Marie Jeanne found herself very quickly and severely punished by the old lady, who was a carbon copy of the priest when it came to discipline and emotion.

She was often stripped naked and whipped and sent her to bed without any supper if the old lady found so much as a speck of dust in any of the rooms Marie Jeanne had been made to clean. The child would also get beaten and starved if she cried for her mother or siblings.

Every morning she would walk to a nearby convent to attend sewing classes as she was to be apprenticed as a seamstress. Following a full day sewing, she would hurry home to a cold *talo*, a corn cake resembling a tortilla, and a half glass of milk, before she would clean the lady's house, sweep the hearth, run errands, and help the cook prepare meals. Marie Jeanne soon learned her place in the household and learned to hold back tears – they were never allowed to fall. The little girl was eight years old.

The young cook who was also an apprentice felt so sorry for the child that she would sometimes hold out a small bit of food for her. They had to be very careful so the lady of the house would not notice; she kept an eagle eye on what was consumed and she was a very frugal and mean person, although, she herself ate well and only the best. She would sometimes reward the young ones with an extra bit of *talo* or even a piece of cheese or an egg. But these foods were very expensive, and though the woman was well-to-do, she didn't want to waste them on good-for-nothing children.

Once in a while, Marie Jeanne was allowed to go home because the priest was expecting a visit from his brother. This was always a happy occasion for her, for she loved her Dad very much and from him learned many wonderful and joyful things. He told her stories of her homeland, her family history and background, and taught her the old songs that were sung by the *chaharrac,* or the old folks.

Much to the chagrin of Don Cruz, Santiago taught his small daughter the Basque dances. As he himself was known as a good dancer, he delighted in Marie Jeanne's ability. Of course, the monsignor's eye promised instant and fierce punishment after her father's visit. Still Marie Jeanne treasured these few visits and gladly suffered the beatings that followed these rare chances to dance and to spend a few minutes with her beloved father.

Subsequently, upon her return to the old woman's home, she would be punished if she was caught singing or dancing.

Before every evening meal, the lady would pull up a rocker, take her very large cat on her lap, remove heavy wooden carved beads from the hook by the fireplace and made the child kneel on the cold floor where they would proceed to say the rosary in a pious way to atone for any sins committed during the day. (Marie Jeanne was of the opinion that the lady should have spent most of her life on her knees.)

To the hungry child, this time seemed such an awful eternity, for she would receive a swift kick if her stomach rumbled, distracting her thoughts from the recitation. All the while, the cat sat on the lady's lap glaring ever so balefully at Marie Jeanne. If she even opened an eye, she thought the cat would make the old woman aware of it and she would be reprimanded. She hated the cat with a passion because it always seemed to be staring at her. She imagined that the cat looked at her like she was a succulent mouse. The cat, of course, shared the woman's table and bed at night. It received the best of food instead of a *talo* and a pallet in the kitchen such as was Marie Jeanne's lot.

The child remained sleepless half the night due to the rumblings of her stomach, for in this house the table was meager. Even with the appetite of Don Cruz, the table at home had not been sparse. The old woman and her cat managed to consume all the food that had been prepared. Any scraps left over the cat would get.

Marie Jeanne missed her Mama, her brothers, and sisters and she longed for the outside where the birds sang and the flowers bloomed and where the dark old house and its musty cat smell did not exist. It seemed that the smell of the animal persisted in the house despite the child's vigorous tries at getting rid of it and it caused her hatred of the cat to grow even stronger.

One day, the old woman left the house to go visiting, after sharply admonishing Marie Jeanne to have the parlor shining clean before she returned. The girl went to work with rags and polish, all the while being watched by her nemesis: the cat. All of a sudden, Marie Jeanne's wild imagination took over and the cat became something evil. The woman became one of the *sorgiñas,* or witches in the stories her brother Louis was always telling her, and the cat became her *familiar*. It was not hard to imagine the pointed, hairy chin of the old woman and the dark night color of the black cat.

For a moment, her mind seemed to snap, and snatching the heavy wooden rosary off the wall she proceeded to beat the living daylights out of the animal. The poor terrified cat leaped about the room, trying to climb the drapes to escape the rosary beads which must have been very painful for the poor animal which had never received so much as a cuff in its entire life.

Marie Jeanne came to her senses and was horrified to think she had offended God by using the beads in such a way. She fully expected to be struck dead at any moment.

That night, as was usual, the woman took the cat on her lap, reached for the rosary and the cat went berserk! It howled, jumped and screeched, trying to evacuate the room in a hurry. The cat clawed its mistress severely and hid under the bed. No doubt about it, some evil force had entered her home and entered her cat. She went to the village priest who agreed that the cat would need to be destroyed because the devil had possessed it.

Marie Jeanne, feeling badly, enlisted the help of Louis, who turned the cat out, miles from the house. Evidently, the poor pampered cat did not survive on its own, for it was never seen again and rumors were heard (I feel sure instigated by my Uncle Louis, and made worse by his embellishments), about a black witch that lived in the woods who stole the souls of the unwary who carried on her shoulder a large black cat, who had very peculiar scars on him.

Meanwhile, the old lady never touched the rosary again, instead praying on her knees at the side of her bed, for she was not at all sure that the rosary beads were to be reckoned with.

Marie Jeanne had at least one consolation. Even though the woman never changed her penurious ways and beat the child regularly, Marie Jeanne's brother Louis on his frequent visits would often crouch beneath the woman's bedroom window and pretend to be a yowling black cat. How the two of them chortled as they watched her jump into her bed and pull the covers up to her pointed nose. She never realized how much the visits of the cat coincided with those of Louis.

A few months after the cat episode, Louis came to take Marie Jeanne home. The young cook, having served her apprenticeship, had then returned to her home and told her parents about the treatment the child endured with Madame. They offered Marie Jeanne another apprenticeship with their kinfolk who ran a hotel and cafe in Baigorri (Baigorry in French).

Hurriedly, Marie Jeanne and Louis scampered through the woods after throwing Marie Jeanne's belongings into a cloth bag. They wanted to get out of the woods before the *gatu beltza* (or black cat) got them. Marie Jeanne always believed the horror stories Louis told her, just as most small Basque children believe in hauntings, witches, and *laminak,* which are trolls or evil spirits who live in the country. They are very hard to control, taking on any shape or form they desire and, along with witches, can do a great deal of harm to anyone who has angered them. Marie Jeanne firmly believed that she had angered more than one troll in her short life.

Louis told her about the time he had been fishing and the black witch, who'd been gathering tadpoles for her brew, had threatened him and shouted at him angrily. Not wishing to be turned into a black dog or a frog, he had left his catch on the bank and ran away. (I'm sure Petra, the gypsy, had a nice fish dinner that evening). In any case, gullible Marie Jeanne believed every one of his stories.

Marie Jeanne's sister, Pauline, had been sent to a distant relative (at the ripe age of twelve), who had married well and moved to Paris. Pauline became a "nanny" for the couple's two children because the parents wanted the children to grow up with the Basque language and culture and there was a substantial wage for Don Cruz's pockets.

Pauline spent some time with this family and did not have to suffer any hardships as she had with other "hosts."

My aunt Pauline told me once that these two children were the most incorrigible, spoiled brats she had ever had the misfortune to meet. She said they knew so many bad words in French and Basque that they sometimes mortified her.

At the end of Pauline's stint in Paris, her relative gave her a very large gift, which she was not to tell about at home. A large sum of money was put into an account for her because the couple was well aware of the situation at home. She was to use it only for an emergency or keep it as a dowry for when she was married. She used it to thumb her nose at Uncle Cruz when she was finally able to escape his clutches and come to America when brother Louis sent for her.

Meanwhile, Mary Jeanne was once again apprenticed to a large hotel in Baigorri and found herself under the good hands of a master chef. Her class room was the large, busy, and hot hotel kitchen. Here, she learned haute cuisine as well as every day workingmen's fare and on her visits home she was plied with all the good food she could carry for herself and her family.

These people were very familiar with Uncle Cruz and his big hands and huge appetite. Almost everyone in the small towns surrounding Banca was familiar with the bad situation at the Goyhenetche home, but sometimes closing their eyes was the best way to handle it. There is a saying in the Basque country that says, "*ikhusten ezdien begiak ezdu eguiten bate nigarric,*" much the same as turning a blind eye.

Uncle Cruz would have looked perfectly at home with his big heavy hands clutched around jail bars, but even today older Basques look on the clergy with much the same respect and reverence, often closeing their eyes to any infallibility.

As time passed, Marie Jeanne's brothers drifted off to jobs in other towns and other countries. Domingo and Francisco went to the forests to become woodcutters. Jean Pierre, Marie Jeanne's youngest brother, was killed in a hunting accident. He was an avid hunter and kept the family larder full of game. One day while hunting hares, he accidentally shot himself in the stomach when he slipped and fell with the loaded gun. He was found later in the day and carried down the mountainside to medical help, but he died soon after. Jean Pierre was only fifteen years old at the time. He had been a kind and gentle boy who had often been the brunt of the monsignor's wrath. Marie Jeanne named her youngest son Jean Pierre after him, but he was always known as Pete.

Uncle Louis came to the United States to become a sheepherder, like so many before him. Louis was the prankster in the family and his ability to laugh and make jokes often kept him out of serious problems when one of his jokes would backfire. He would pull on his sisters long black hair and make her laugh, but he could sure make her mad as quick as a wink too. When he made enough money, he sent for his sisters. Aunt Pauline was the first to go. This left only Marie Jeanne and her little sister Catherine at home.

One day, her brother Domingo lost an eye and part of his hand in a logging accident. He came home to live and became an accomplished smuggler. Knowing all the roads, pathways, ravines and hills very well from boyhood, he was never caught but had many close calls. He often had to ditch his entire contraband load to escape, but he managed to get a pretty good living out of it. I suppose it was a pretty good way to get back at Uncle Cruz and his authority and must have been a good slap in the face for his demanded respect.

Grandfather Goyhenetche passed away and Mama said although he had never been diagnosed, he probably had suffered from diabetes for some time.

Aita Haundia, Don Cruz, passed away in his sleep. Marie Jeanne thought he literally exploded during one of his pigouts on *murcillas* or blood sausage. Rich foods were his downfall and though he had been warned by his doctor many times, he could not curtail his eating.

The people of the town always shared with the clergy at butchering time and brought him the very best of their bounty. The finest sausages, *murcillas*, and richest hams came Don Cruz's way. Grandmama, who was an excellent cook in her own right, prepared chickens, ducks, geese, succulent veal, and baked goods for him. He ate and ate and continued to eat until he ate himself to death.

The black cat came in handy one more time in Marie Jeanne's life, this time with the priest. One day, her mother had made a beautiful crème brûlée for Uncle Cruz, and put it in the window to cool. Marie Jeanne, being hungry, consumed it all and spent the rest of the day in the hayloft hiding from the priest, feeling nauseated and sick with her chores undone. Anticipating the sharp slaps she would get from her "favorite" Uncle Cruz, she vomited up all that fabulous crème brûlée!

Everyone was told that the cream pudding had been eaten by a large black cat. When Uncle Louis and Pauline sent money and summoned Marie Jeanne to the states, she sadly confessed to her mother that she was the black cat in the crème episode. Grandmama told her she had known all along, but she still wished that the little, black kitten would stay with her forever.

So with a very sad heart, Marie Jeanne left Grandmama Michaela and France. She was off to America.

Banca. Photo courtesy of Catherine Çaldumbide.

The De Grasse. Photo from Wikipedia.

Off to a land across the sea
To a strange and faraway place
New promises lay beyond the sea
A daring new life to face.
Bravely she met her new wide world
Leaving her past behind
Her home and gentle mother
Closed out of her restless mind
Hiding her tears and a hurting heart
She stared at the setting sun
Never a tear did she let fall
Sharing her misery with none
Telling herself, she didn't hurt at all,
The girl hid her deep emotion,
Stood stone-faced as
The De Grasse *sailed over the ocean.*

"A young man was loading sacks into a wagon, pulled by two huge harnessed horses, the likes of which she had never seen."

THE NEW WORLD

It was with a great deal of fear that she took the train from Baiona (Bayonne) to LeHavre, where she boarded the French ship *De Grasse*. It was a semi cargo and passenger ship that made frequent ports for loading or unloading its cargo. It took forty days to finally dock at the smoky, dismal-looking port of New York City.

Seasick and heartsick as she had been for the majority of the trip, Marie Jeanne's first thoughts were to return to France at the earliest possible chance.

She had been told that money grew on trees in America but she had yet to see any trees. If that were true, brother Louis would have been right in there picking money, and it wouldn't have taken this long to send for her. There must be an "*astelehena azte gusis*," a Monday every week in this country. Perhaps she would be lucky to find only one Monday a week.

She was sent to Valentin Aguirre's hotel for Basques. He saw to it that she got on the train the next day with a tag around her neck that said Ely, Nevada. Still feeling sick with all her hopes and dreams shattered, she sat back in her seat on the great lumbering and noisy train.

She had been put into the hands of a porter-conductor who saw to it that she had meals and that she made the right connections to arrive at her destination. She was very grateful for his help as he spoke a little French and as he saw her utter distress. He brought her treats which she could not eat. He tried to see to her every comfort, but the little "mamzelle," as he called her, seemed to be afraid of him.

This was her first encounter with a black man and she was fascinated by his totally dark skin. She wondered if a witch had turned him black until she saw many more of his kind. It seemed that America was made up of many colors, many new experiences, and, hopefully, rewarding new sights and opportunities. She was so looking forward to seeing her brother again, for their homeland had never been the same after he left Banca.

Soon, the train was rumbling its noisy, smelly way over the countryside and she found herself marveling at the panoramic changes for mile after mile. She saw many villages, huge sprawling smoky cities, sparkling wide rivers, and rolling plains of *ogia*, or wheat fields. She glimpsed wooden pens holding thousands of cattle, sheep, and hogs. Once she even saw an open air market much like the one in Donibane Garazi (St. Jean Pied de Port) and she swallowed the lump in her throat as pictures of home swam before her eyes.

Soon she was surrounded by towering mountains with steep and rocky sides and she giggled to herself, just a little, as she pictured Louis trying to climb one of these monsters or rolling the huge boulders down into the deep canyons. He would be full of spirited jokes and ghostly stories and would probably pull her hair and make her so mad.

A silent tear slid down her cheek and she quickly brushed it away, lest someone should see.

The sudden white expanse that filled her eyes was explained to her as being a large deposit of salt. She was amazed by the scene.

She suddenly thought of the many times she had deliberately oversalted her "kind uncle's" soup. She could really have gotten the old boy going with this much salt. Then she quickly crossed herself because it was bad to speak of the dead in that manner. She could still see him at the pulpit with bulging eyes and fat stomach, delivering one of his long sermons and bellowing at the congregation. She shivered.

Putting those thoughts out of her mind, she marveled at the size of this country and wondered what was in store for her future. She knew, with almost a certainty, she would never see her Mother's face again. She quickly swallowed the tears that came to smart her eyes.

Then, the train stopped at a dusty little town. A sign on one of the buildings proclaimed that this was Currie, Nevada.

She could see a few houses, a place that said HOTEL, and a livery stable, where she could see a young man who was loading sacks into a wagon that was pulled by two huge harnessed horses, the likes of which she had never seen.

The black porter came, took her luggage to a little bit of a platform and beckoned her to follow. He said, in his fractured French, "Ici Mamzelle, is your destination," and he smiled at her, touched his cap, and said "Adieu." The train roared off into the distance with a mournful cry and belching black smoke as it disappeared from her bewildered sight.

A short, heavyset man with a white apron over his more than ample belly came toward her and spoke to her in Spanish. She understood him to say he was named Manuel Edo and she was to follow him, but she rebelled furiously and yelled in Basque that she was "damned" if she was going to follow anybody. Her destination was Ely and she was going to Ely and that was that!

By now, her famous temper had taken over and

she began to kick at her luggage until her toes stung, all the while flinging implications that she most certainly had never learned at the knees of her Uncle Cruz.

Someone behind her cleared his throat and she met the startling blue eyes and the amused gaze of the man who had been loading the wagon. He approached her very cautiously and spoke to her in Basque. His reddish brown hair and very blue eyes held her attention, for he certainly did not look like most of the Basques she was acquainted with. Besides, he had a half mocking smile that infuriated her already ruffled feelings.

He explained to her that if she was Marie Jeanne from Banca, that there had been a change of plans. She was to stay in Currie and help Gregoria Mariluch at the hotel because her little daughter had been taken ill. Louis had informed them that Marie Jeanne was coming and she could stay and help until Louis could pick her up.

The young man told her that he was Arnaud Paris, born in Lasa (Lasse), France, and that he knew her brother and sister very well. In fact, Pauline had been a girlfriend until she up and married his good friend Pete Etcheverry.

In an effort to calm Marie Jeanne, he related the very recent escapade that Louis had carried out. Lous had taken his donkey up the hotel steps to his room and left him there for the day. Of course, the animal raised a very big commotion and kicked the heck out of everything. It had cost Louis a small fortune to placate the maid, who made Louis clean up the mess, and to pay for the donkey's damage to the room.

Marie Jeanne laughed until tears flooded her eyes, and agreed that Louis was indeed an "enfant terrible," although she was never surprised at anything her brother did.

The young man took her luggage to the hotel, introducing her to the Mariluch family, then drove off with his big and frightening horses. They threw up clods of dirt and rocks with their huge feet and their rolling huge eyes frightened her so bad that she realized she had not thanked him for helping her. In her misery, she raised a hand in Adieu when he looked back at the lonely forlorn little Basque girl standing in the dusty street. This was the first encounter with the man who was to become her beloved husband.

None of Marie Jeanne's brothers ever married, but Aunt Pauline had married just before Marie Jeanne arrived, to a man named Pete Etcheverry (Big Pete). Thay would have a family of six children. Uncle Pete passed away while still young and Aunt Pauline raised two sons and four daughters by herself. My cousins – Gentty, Alice, Albert, Elizabeth, Lois Ann, and Frances – grew up in a strict but loving home with only a Mother, for Aunt Pauline never remarried.

Marie Jeanne married Arnaud Paris and they had Arnaud, Mike, John, Pete, and me. She became

Mama Marie.

Never very mellow and responsive, Mama became strict and limited her love. She always treated her boys with a different manner, although she was not overly emotional with them either. They got their share of slaps and recriminations at times, for Mama was always quick with the back of her hand, but it was always, it seemed to me, my back that caught her slap and the brunt of her temper (boy, did she ever have one), and it was I who was expected to excel at whatever I did. The boys could slide a little but not the girl.

Oh, what a difference there was between the relationship between our Dad and I and that of Mama and I.

Aita never loved with restrictions. He gave us all unconditional love. He was capable of putting his arms around us and showing us that he cared. Mama never could.

Sometimes, Aita would yell and administer a slap to the unwary behind, but it was always given with love. I never was the recipient of these slaps and felt very privileged. I never felt deprived, for Mama had plenty of slaps to go around.

Currie Depot

Currie Hotel

Currie, Nevada

What mattered the love in a mother's heart if it was hidden
behind a wall?
If enough of that love she could not impart to answer a
daughter's call
What mattered the voice of the crying child who reached
out in hopeful despair
Hopes and dreams never quite met with the love that was
hidden there
What mattered if the body was clothed and fed but the
heart felt shattered and torn
And pushed aside where it lay and bled seeking love
perhaps never born
What mattered was the love in the father's eye who gave
that ever wanting need
Who never left the soul of the child to die and never left the
heart to bleed
It matters that love runs through this tale like a silvery
fragile thread
It matters that life and each path she took was where her
father led
He answered the small child's questions with a truth and
patience unmeasured
With an open heart, he gave his all, with a love she always
treasured

Wedding party. Standing, left to right: Mike Camino, Louie Goyhenetche, and Marianna Camino. Seated: Marie Jeanne and Arnaud Paris

THE WIFE

Marie Jeanne remained at Currie for quite a while. She became friends with Gregoria, the owner of the hotel. She helped with cooking, cleaning, and caring of the children. Gregoria was a very warm-hearted, loving, and kind person who instantly took the young girl to her heart; they formed a friendship that was to last a lifetime. Gregoria lifted the curtain of homesickness from the shoulders of the girl and became like a mother to her. In a very warm way she gave Marie Jeanne a glimpse of what her life would be like in the states. She also satisfied Marie Jeanne's curiosity about the young man who had made such an impression on her. Gregoria told Marie Jeanne that this man was a good and kind person. He had a very good sense of humor and could sing and tell stories and poems with the best. Marie Jeanne wondered aloud if she would ever see Arnaud again, and Gregoria was quick to assure her that he often came to Currie for supplies.

Marie Jeanne came to love Gregoria and never forgot the kindly woman and her advice, always holding her in high esteem.

Sometime later, Louis came to Currie to pick up his little sister and what a joyous, tearful reunion they had! Both had a lifetime of tears and love and excitement to look forward to. Of course, Louis had to pull her hair, whirl her around and generally make her quite annoyed with some of his dirtiest stories and his teasing. She was so happy to see him that she now forgave him just about anything.

She asked about the young man who had helped her in Currie and how she had forgotten to thank him but was very quickly reassured that she would probably see him in Eureka where she was originally scheduled to work for Louis's good friends, Mike and Jeanne Etchegaray, who owned the Basque hotel there.

In Eureka, she was warmly greeted by her employers. Marie Jeanne had known Jeanne from Europe and was very soon incorporated into operations at the very busy hotel.

At that time, Eureka was the hub of the cattle and the sheep industry and Marie Jeanne found no time to reflect on the past. She rose at four in the morning and often found herself still busy at midnight. On weekends, generally, the boys would come into town

The Eureka Hotel, Eureka, Nevada

from the ranches and sheep camps and there would be gatherings and dances. Many times she found herself still dancing at four in the morning, so she would put on a clean apron and start fixing breakfast for all the revelers. She had to cook three meals a day, help with the maid work for the hotel, and help Jeanne do the shopping. For this, she was paid thirty dollars a month with room and board. She had very little time to do anything but work, so she certainly enjoyed those dances, which she could now do without the wrathful eye of Don Cruz watching her every move. People said that Marie Jeanne could dance on water!

She managed to repay her brother for her passage from France. It was a custom for a brother or sister who came to the states to pay *pasaya saria,* or payment of passage for any siblings that wanted to come to America to live.

There was a quota of how many immigrants could stay. Those from Spain were worse off than the French because they could only stay three years with a guarantee of employment from the stockman who had hired them. Unless they married a citizen, they were not allowed to stay.

Her heart was often heavy and she had to fight back her tears and put on a "good" face for those around her. She seldom saw her family, for Louis was back at the sheep camp and Pauline was now expecting her first child so did not venture far from home.

Marie Jeanne despaired of learning English. If she tried to say it like it looked (some words looked a lot like French words), people would be sure to laugh and she hated to be put in the position of having someone laugh at her.

One morning, Mike, her boss, bet her a month's wages she could not go to the store and bring back a pair of shoes and something for breakfast. With a great deal of pointing and waving of her sandals, which she removed from her foot, she did manage to bring back a pair of white shoes, a jug of milk, a dozen eggs, a box of corn flakes, and a can of peaches. She had purposefully brought back more than Mike had stipulated for fear that he would renege. Besides, he never said the shoes had to fit. Mike, who was a good-natured man, cheerfully paid his bet, but he never underestimated Marie Jeanne again.

Many young men came to court her, as a young pretty girl was never single for long. The young men were lonely and hungered for female companionship, like young stags in a herd of deer. If they'd had horns, there would have been a lot of clashing, I'm sure. There were arguments and fisticuffs. Although she was friendly to many, none of them managed to capture her heart. She was very popular at the dances and parties. She had a lovely singing voice, danced like the wind, and could play the harmonica while dancing. Her rippling, long black hair, usually kept in a bun while working, was released to below her waist, and it, along with her pretty red cheeks and snapping black eyes, added to the young girl's appeal to the young bucks.

One young fellow in particular had just purchased a new car and was earnestly pursuing Marie Jeanne, trying to impress her with his wealth. Cars in those days were very expensive and he was so proud of his achievement that he would not let any other young man near it. This fellow happened to be very selfish and egotistical and the other boys resented it.

Uncle Louis, in particular, resented the attention this young man paid his sister and, disliking him intensely anyway, was very jealous of the car. He could not buy one and could not have driven if he'd had the money for the purchase.

After one of the dances, Uncle Louis collected a big boxful of fresh manure, smeared it all over the car, opened the door and decorated the back seat. When the man came out to his car, he turned on his former object of affection, Marie Jeanne, and accused her of putting her brother up to this. Her famous temper soared, she boxed both his ears soundly, then turned on her brother and boxed his too. She gave both of them a tongue-lashing they would never forget.

It was a very meek Louis who once more had a nasty mess to clean and an angry woman to placate. He could not stop her from kicking his shins sharply and hitting him with anything she could pick up. Finally, he ran for all he was worth from the mad woman who was, by then, brandishing an iron skillet. Everyone laughed at the sight of tough, hell-bent, devil-may-care Louis Goyhenetche running for his life in front of an angry woman and her frying pan. Luckily, she gave up the chase or he would have had a bashing for sure. Then she turned her total attention to the hapless man with the dirty car. She told him what to do with his affection and his manured car, kicked him several times, and got him to running in front of her frying pan. She slung it at him, barely missing his head, to prove her point. It was the end of a very one-sided romance.

One day, after a particularly hot day in the kitchen, Marie Jeanne peeped into the dining room and there at one of the tables was the young man who had helped her in Currie. It seems that he had never been far from her mind in any case. At the same time, the young man looked up and, seeing her, realized that the delicious meal he had just consumed had been prepared by the girl that had made such a sad picture in Currie.

It had always been his custom to come to town every few weeks from the sheep camp to have a home cooked meal at the hotel and to play a game or two of *mus*, which is a card game that is played in the Basque Country. (A better name for it would be bluff—he who bluffs best wins the game.)

Marie Jeanne came out to speak to him and finally thanked him for helping her when she arrived. She thought to herself, he has a very beautiful lopsided smile and two deep dimples that appear when his intense sky-blue eyes twinkle. His hair was almost auburn and he looked very different from most of the other young Basques, who were usually dark-haired. Her own brothers were dark and Louis had the nickname of "*Banca Beltza*," which meant black man from Banca. Arnaud also appeared to be a bit shy and would let a smile speak for him instead of words or the incessant bragging of so many of the others.

Arnaud asked Marie Jeanne to dance later on, and from there on he was her only partner. Together, the two of them were quite the dancing team and found out later that night during the celebration that they sang very beautifully together. It is the Basque style at such gatherings to challenge each other in song or poems. These verses are known as *bertziak,* and Arnaud was a natural poet. In any case, his fair good looks complimented her dark beauty and everyone commented on how well they looked together.

They danced the night away and everyone could see the lay of the land. After a few more dates, they found themselves deeply in love. They wanted to spend their lives together.

Arnaud and Marie Jeanne were married in the early part of spring. It was a well-attended, beautifully catered wedding and people came from miles around to dance and enjoy the ceremony uniting the popular couple.

The caterer was Maria Echevarria from Ely. She was a warm and wonderful lady who Arnaud had been acquainted with for some years. She and her husband John "Lequito" (nicknamed for the town in the Spanish Basque Country [Lekeitio] that he came from), became such good friends that the couple was always part of our family. Marie Jeanne and Maria often catered weddings and funerals together afterward and, when I was born, she became my beloved godmother and became known as Amatchi to the whole family. She was a great joy for all of us and Amatchi to all. Her daughter, Marie (Ordoqui), and son, Peter (Echevarria), were godparents to my youngest brother Pete.

All of the Paris kids thought that Amatchi was a very special person. When my Father became so very ill and was on his death-bed, Maria came from Ely to help, to be there, to comfort, and to love. What a wonderful, giving person she was. I am certain that God has a special spot in Heaven for her.

Lequito was a jewel among the rarest of jewels. He would play with us, gave such wonderful horseback rides, and tried to show us how to blow up muscles by sticking our thumbs in our mouths and blowing very hard. He said if you blew hard enough, you would have muscles like Popeye. But as hard as we blew, which at times was enough to bring on a mild headache, we could never blow a muscle. Lequito could do it though. We were always amazed at his hard muscles and thought of him as "superguy," as indeed he was. I can just picture him up in Heaven, surrounded by all the little angels, teaching them how to blow Popeye muscles and following him everywhere for horse back rides. What a very happy and wonderful family to be a part of.

Within a few days, the young Paris couple went to their new home, which was, for the first summer, an old line camp in a one-room cabin in Secret Pass in Elko County, where the sheep were. Later on when the herds had to move to new grazing, Marie Jeanne learned to harness the big horses she had thought so fearful, hitch them to the sheep wagon, and move the camp from feeding ground to feeding ground on the trails to winter camping. Through the summer, though, they stayed in the Ruby Mountains, moving occasionally, and very soon the big horses became excellent friends, responding to her commands and nosing her pockets for the sugar cubes she kept for them.

Despite their large size and worrisome looks, she soon found them to be very fascinating companions. She would talk to them as if they were human, while they pulled the big heavy camp that was her home with all her belongings. She felt at home.

Every day was a hardworking day for the young

Looking toward Secret Pass, Ruby Mountains, Nevada

bride. She would bake the bread in huge round Dutch ovens for the rest of the sheep camps, digging the pits where the ovens were placed in the ground and hauling the wood for the fires. She washed the other sheepherders' clothes, hauling water for the task, and scrubbed them on a *latzaharria,* or washboard, even ironing them with a couple of flat irons that she had received for a wedding present and which she had to heat on the stove. Brother Louis said she could now use the flat irons to bean somebody instead of a cast iron skillet.

She cooked gourmet meals of *chilindron,* or Dutch oven lamb meat and potatoes, pots of savory beans, and stew, She always had a hot meal on the back of the stove when her tired and hungry husband would come "home." Of course, there was never enough room on the little stove to really show culinary expertise, but the camp meals were very satisfying to her loving husband who adored his young wife so very much.
Sometimes, it was a very exhausted young bride that fell heavily into her bed at night and nestled happily in the arms of her proud and happy husband, for too soon the dawn would break and it would be time to start a new day.

To their delight, Marie Jeanne found herself pregnant very quickly; Arnaud used to say she was pregnant in the first two hours after their wedding.

She knew her husband would make a wonderful father to their children because she saw the way their friends' little ones loved him and she herself was very fond of children and was looking forward to having her very own.

Then one day, she slipped off the tongue of the sheep wagon and Arnaud had barely enough time to rush her to Ely before my brother Arnaud Santiago was prematurely born, weighing a little over four pounds. He was sickly and puny, and allergic to Mama's milk. What a frightening start for the first of their family. He soon rallied from the shock of the traumatic birth for he was a real tough scrapper. It wasn't long before they took him to his camp home followed by his own herd of milking goats for his supply. Their friends teased them about the timeframe between the marriage and the birth, but they just chuckled and were so grateful that their pride and joy was fine and the "spittin" image of his proud Aita. Anyway, Aita used to say that the first one can come anytime but the second would take nine months.

Now, whenever the camp moved, everyone who saw it knew that it belonged to Arnaud and Marie Jeanne, for he had put a cord along both sides and the back of the camp, and on this cord, every morning, Marie Jeanne hung the baby diapers to dry. Scrubbed "hospital white" and disinfected by a day in the sun, those diapers flapped merrily in the wind, proclaiming to all who saw it that here was a true shepherds' castle with a little prince inside, being pulled down the countryside by two big draft horses, followed by three milking goats and an Australian shepherd dog.

Queenie, the shepherd, was Marie Jeanne's constant companion and faithful babysitter; not only the first child but to all of us in turn, I think she considered us as her "pups." Aita had found her, tiny and starving, where someone had dropped her and she was quickly nursed back to health by the young woman who had never been allowed to own a pet in her life.

Queenie quickly learned that when the baby was put in the washtub on blankets, it was her job to watch the baby and not allow anything or anyone near it.

When she had her first litter in the old shed, Marie Jeanne put the little boy in the tub and called her dog. She came willingly, but then was torn between her own family and her human baby. She ran back and forth between babies until she figured a solution for herself. She hurried to the shed and brought her six puppies and laid them on the blankets beside the sleeping boy where she took care of all of them at once. I believe that was her smallest litter, for it always seemed she had ten pups at a time.

When I was little, I spent many happy hours tumbling and playing with her pups. She was our loyal friend and the mother to so many of our sheep dogs. Bred to male border collies, her pups were some of the best sheep dogs in the country, very much in demand by the other sheep men. I always got in a lot of trouble too because playing with the pups got me very filthy and always made Mama mad. Oh well, no matter what I did Mama was always mad at me anyway.

Everyone always tried to tell me that if you played with pups too much, you could spoil them and take away their ability to adapt to herding life. Phooey! Some of the best pups turned out to be the best sheep dogs, and they were the ones I played with the most.

Queenie did not mind my playing with her pups for she so often played with us. Unfortunately, the puppies were weaned from her at an early age and given to the herders to train. They learned very quickly by following the herders and the older dogs so their puppy life was short indeed. Poor Queenie would promptly have another litter and start all over again. She always seemed so sad when the pups were removed but she immediately replaced them until she was quite old.

Eighteen months after Arnaud, my brother Mike arrived. He was a whopping thirteen pounds and Aita used to say he was born half-raised. Mama swore she carried him eleven months for, according to her calculations, he was supposed to have been born in March. So much for the theory of Dad's that the second one would take nine months.

Mike was a good baby, being very placid and

hearty, eating well, and sleeping all night almost from birth. He was the complete opposite of his older brother, who was always on the run and very high-strung. Where Arnaud was a "doer," Mike was content to sit and watch. His Mama doted on him and the rest of us were always aware that Mike was her favorite child. When I was born, eighteen months later, he made his first attempt to walk. When she could no longer carry him, his philosophy that he didn't need to walk, because Mama would carry, him was drastically changed.

Now, there were three babies and a triple workload. I was just what was needed on Mama's agenda. She figured she was happy with two boys but here was another demanding baby, and a girl at that. Aita was happy with his ever-increasing family, but I think Mama had enough on her plate.

Her girlhood was by then behind her, her time as a young wife was behind her, and she became My Mama Marie.

During the time we were babies, we stayed in the sheep camp with the herds. The big wagon was our home. Being a child in a moving home will always be a good memory for me. Our life really made for togetherness and family unity. We had no cribs or bassinettes and all slept in the big bed, with the boys relegated to the foot and the baby in the middle.

Sometime in the next four years, our parents must have come to the conclusion that there were too many babies in the bed and Mama was pregnant with her fourth child, for Dad went on a trip because he wanted to buy a ranch. He purchased the Forest Home cattle ranch in Sunnyside, Nevada. By the time John and Pete were born, we had become both cattle and sheep ranchers.

We had a big log house with six bedrooms, a huge kitchen, a combination living room-dining room, and a big porch that went all around the front and side of the house. The upper part of the log house had never been finished so Aita made a stair case and divided off the top part into four new bedrooms and also piped water into the house from the little stream that ran through the ranch. We heated water for our baths and cleaning in a big tank located on the side of the huge kitchen stove.

We had no bathroom facilities but, never having had one, we thought the "two-holer" outhouse was a very fine one, and what a convenience.

Whenever I had to go at night, I was always too afraid of the dark to go. Preferring to put everything on hold until daytime, my brother Arnaud was finally given the job of taking me to the outhouse. He always accompanied me with his flashlight, for this was his time to get me.

He would light my way and wait outside making animal sounds and howling like coyotes and, never being sure it was Arnaud making all those noises, I was too afraid to go anyway. Of course, he always denied hearing a darn thing but on the way back home, carefully lighting my way, he would tell me horror stories, tuck me back into bed, and drop a casual remark about the big "Mamoo" or monster that lurked under one's bed and ate up everything that was not covered. Needless to say, I would huddle under the covers, afraid to even stick my head out, near suffocated at times, always so afraid of the Mamoo. Even today, I do not sleep well if I am not covered at least by the sheet. I am still a big baby about going out in the dark by myself. What a number he did on me. But, he was still my hero, for no one else would be responsible for me getting to the bathroom at night and I believed his stories with all my heart.

I always hated Halloween and believed in witches and monsters and ghosts until I would scare myself silly.

I slept in the second bed in my parents room with my new brother, but he was such a colicky crying baby that Aita and Mama decided to put me upstairs and put him in his own bed. I immediately began to have ferocious nightmares that kept the whole family awake, which made a furious mess of my poor Mama, who would rush upstairs, shake me violently awake, pound on me for a while, then give up and slap me a few more times, and dared me to make another peep for the whole night. Of course, that would leave me afraid to go back to sleep so I would lay awake the rest of the night.

Often, Aita would come upstairs and soothe me back to sleep. A lot of times, upon waking in the early morning, he would still be there on my bed, sound asleep: the poor tired man. What a saint that man was to take time for his poor suffering little daughter. He never slapped or even recriminated in any way for having had his own rest wrecked by me almost every night.

I honestly don't know if I was more terrified by my nightmares or Mama's rude awakenings. No sooner would she finish her bout with me, when Baby John would awaken and add his screams to the melee and she'd be off on round number two of her interesting nights. It sure was funny that when Aita put me gently back to sleep, the dreams never recurred.

Mama always mumbled that I was possessed by the Devil and was put into the world just to test her patience. I don't see how because she had no patience to test. It's a wonder that my father ever survived the battles between my Mama and me.

It's here again, and yet again, the dream the bad, bad dream
I cannot move, I cannot breathe, no, I can only
scream and scream.
The figure bending over me with flowing hair and fiery eyes
Is it the one I know or is it not, is it the monster in disguise?
It picks me up and shakes me hard and flings me into the air

It's going to take me from my bed into its
dark and musky lair.
It's going to make a meal of me, of that I'm very sure
Its claws are sinking in my throat, the agony
I cannot endure.
Then suddenly, I'm snatched away, there are soft fingers
in my hair
I'm saved again, the monster is gone and I know
that Aita is there.

Mama was a very tough, formidable person when she was provoked and angry. It certainly was not hard to provoke her, for I could do it just by being in her way sometimes.

Once, when we were still living at the sheep camp, she had been very busy baking bread, having hauled a great load of wood, after putting her small sons to sleep for a nap, and had a great pot of Dutch oven stew going for the evening meal. She had already baked a few breads and was waiting for the ones in her pit to bake. She put a few fresh baked loaves outside on a table to cool, covering them with snowy white flour-sack dish cloths. She was about to lay down beside her sons for a little rest, when she glanced out the cabin window and saw someone coming down the mountainside. She was instantly cautious, for no one ever came from that direction; there were no roads and the mountain was rather steep. The old cabin was very isolated and they seldom had any company here.

She called Queenie in, slammed the door, pushed the old iron bed against it, and got a rifle! Sensing her fear, the dog stood backed against her legs, hackles raised, but did not utter a sound knowing that a gun in hand was bad news.

By now, she could see a large limping man, approaching the old cabin. He seemed to have been burned black by the sun and she saw that he was stark naked! He was wild-eyed and long haired, with his body crisscrossed with many cuts from his journey through the brushy country.

Sniffing the air like an animal, he took a long drink from the water bucket that was hung on the cabin, took two large loaves of Mama's bread and limped away from the old cabin without making a move toward the startled occupants. He was found a day later by the Sheriff's posse, who had been combing the hills for him. He still had a good half loaf of bread and refused to go anywhere until he finished it. He had apparently escaped from an asylum in Colorado and had been trying to make it to the coast, fighting his way over the rough country-side and mountains in his efforts.

Mama said it was a good thing her bread had been *koska,* or heavy and cranky, that day, because it slowed the man down enough for the posse to catch him.

When Aita came home, she told him the story. He had no doubt she would have shot the man to protect her babies and home, except, he explained to her, you had to put the bullets in the gun first.

I don't think she would have been able to shoot anyone, but she would have certainly bashed his head in with an iron skillet, given the chance.

One other time, I saw her get mad through and through at a neighbor who somehow threatened her. I don't know what he said or did to her, but he came running out of the house with her big "pig-sticker" almost in his back. This was a large home-made butcher knife that was a very fierce weapon and she was very handy with it.

I look back now, and laugh at the many ways I made my Mama angry. I would crook my face at her back and cross my eyes, but somehow, she always knew. I would get clouted with a warning that my face would freeze that way, and my eyes would stay crossed forever. She had eyes in the back of her head under that bun of hair she wore. She put her hair in a *moina* every morning, pinning it with what I called "two-legged" pins and putting on her no nonsense, no messing around look of severity. At night, she would let it down where it swirled and rippled down past her waist and it softened her face when she sat under a lamp, crocheting with that glorious hair all about her. So it was with dismay that I watched every morning as she confined her lovely locks in a big bun.

After her own coiffure was done, it was my turn. She'd grab a brush and commence to bring order to my wild and unmanageable mane. Of course, I was not blessed with hair like hers. Mine was long, thick, snarled and tangled, and looked more like a horse's tail. My brothers often referred to me as that end of the horse anyway. It hurt terribly to be brushed and I yelled and screamed all through it. I had to bring down her wrath some way, didn't I? She would bring my hair back and make two long braids so tight that my eyebrows would disappear, but it never stayed in confinement very long. I was soon back to looking like the back end of Old Coaly. (Old Coaly being a horse my brothers loved to compare me to the hind end of.) Soon though, our Aita got tired of my whoops and screams and fraying of Mama's nerves. The only way he could have any peace was to cut my hair like he did my brothers.

He sat us all in turn on an old barrel, got out his cutting outfit, and gave us all Moe's, which were neat little round haircuts. I loved mine. At least now I could brush my own hair without whangings from Mama's brush and the new look sure beat the heck out of looking like Old Coaly.

I don't think I was the most appealing child in the world. I preferred overalls or hand-me-down Levis from the boys to the pretty dresses that Mama made from flour sacks. Flour used to come in printed cloth sacks and Mama would look at dresses in the Wards catalog (Monkey Wards, as we used to say), then cut the same dress out of flour sacks and sew them up for me. They were colorful and quite nice, but you had to keep your legs down and you could not climb on things. I ripped up a lot of clothes that way. You could not ride a pet billy goat that way either. I had "Billy," and he was my golden steed. I thought he smelled pretty good, but I was the only one who had that high opinion of him. Mama could never get his stink out of my clothes, but I spent many happy hours on his back just sitting while he ate and browsed.

Mama wanted me to be gentle and dainty and to be a lady. I was not pink and shiny and dimpled. I was big and broad-shouldered, rough, tough, and an incredible tomboy. I just was not dress material and was never the pretty doll she wanted. I stomped around like a big old boy, in my old shoes that I could not tie. I never learned to tie my shoes until I was almost eight years old. I was loud, boisterous, and a troublemaker, and I drove Mama crazy.

Aita always told me not to push my luck and to stop myself before making Mama mad, but by the time I could do it, it was too late.

I would push her to the limit and by the time her eyes flashed and her nostrils flared, I would have inherited a good slapping. My Dad always put up with my wild hair and bad attitude, for he knew I was very different when I was with him and never seemed to get into trouble.

I could never let him go to town without tagging along. He said I helped him a lot with the shopping, but I know I was more of a hindrance.

In the first place, I always got horribly carsick and poor Dad spent a lot of time cleaning me up and his pickup. We spent a lot of time at the creeks or bodies of water we came to so he could clean up his smelly daughter. One day, my godmother told me to make a hole in a lemon and suck on the juice when we were driving. It worked. From that day on, I carried lemons whenever we traveled.

We always packed a lunch (mostly sardines, bread, and pork and beans), and I always got a treat: a large bottle of Nesbitt orange. One day, I threw the bottle out the truck window as we were traveling the road in Pine Valley. Aita screeched the truck to a halt, gave me a gunny sack, and sent me back to where I had thrown out the bottle. He told me to pick up all the other trash I found alongside the road. I picked up the bottle and a lot of other things and sheepishly went to the truck. Dad had a Prince Albert cigarette and was reading a pocket book, waiting patiently while I had my lesson. He said that fifty years from that time, the country would be littered with cans and bottles because people didn't care to keep the country clean and had no pride. He would be appalled if he could see our roadways and highways today. He would have me out there with a gunny sack for sure.

At the ranch, we all had our chores, our own rooms to keep clean, and we were never allowed to throw trash around. We had to keep the creek clean, for that was our drinking and cleaning supply. We would go wading in it sometimes and my brothers always said that the water tasted like something had washed its feet in it, probably was Old Coaly.

My brothers could be so mean to me at times and, being the only girl with no other way to retaliate, I became even meaner. Once, I rounded up their shoes and put them in the creek to soak overnight in a little dam I had hollowed out. Who do you think got the worst of that?

Then it was time for all of us to go to school. Arnaud and Mike had already completed two grades in town, boarding with my Amatchi, but three and four children were too many to board. Dad found a teacher who would come out to the ranch and teach, but first we had to have six children to open the school. A couple of my cousins came to the ranch and a farmer who had a school age daughter, Irene, sent her to our house where she boarded for the week.

Irene became my best friend and companion. Each Monday, she rode her old black mare Belle to the ranch, then would go home on the stage with Mr.

Schoolhouse at the Forest Home Ranch, left to right: Mike Paris and Arnaud Paris

Forest Home Ranch in the White River Valley, White Pine County, Nevada

Stuckey, who brought the mail, on Friday nights. The old mare would be turned loose after bringing Irene and she would just plod on home. It was a distance of eight miles.

Irene's father had a farm and he raised Morgan horses and sold eggs and produce. These animals were special and so very beautiful being well-conformed and expensive animals. It wasn't long until they started foaling long-eared lovely mule colts.

My pet donkey Patchi had come calling and, having an affinity for those appealing young mares, he had himself a grand old time making "Morgan mules." He was uncontrollable, as he could jump any fence in the country, and every chance he got he was over there courting the mares. Finally, though, his wandering ways got the best of him. After one escape he got tangled so badly in a barb-wire fence that he had to be put down. I'm sure Aita purchased most of the mules for the sheep camp from Irene's father. They were from pure-bred mammas.

I remember the times I sat on his back, my long-eared
wonderful "steed":
wild and willful and stubborn – he was a "donkey" indeed
Not a fence in the world would hold him in, flying over all
like a bird
Proclaiming his love at the neighbor's farm for the
beautiful Morgan herd.

Patchi so loved the lovely black mares, never loving a
"donk" of his own
He was cut badly on the fence and later had
to be put down
Alas, finally paid so dearly for the illicit
"oats" he had sown
If only he'd stuck to the donkeys, he'd of
lived to a ripe old age.
In heaven no gates or fences but
Morgans are all over the sage!

Dad hired Gertrude Brown, a teacher who had taught on rural ranches before. She came to us driving her old car and brought her dog Freckles with her. Freckles was quite old and mean, though she treated him like a baby. Between the two of them, they were quite intimidating.

Freckles often looked at me like I was a pork chop or an equally fine cut of meat. In fact, he looked like the dog that haunted my dreams at night and I hated him, having the same aversion to Mrs. Brown.

The teacher would swing her willow stick liberally across my back or my unsuspecting back end, and then report to Mama that I was a blockhead and did not try. Of course, I got a hiding at home for being a donkey. Mrs. Brown prided herself on her harsh methods and the boys caught it just as badly as I did. Even at the dining table, she would show off her teaching by using the willow stick at the table when we could not spell some hideous big word because who could concentrate on anything with that stick in your face?

I thought I got back at her when I spoke to her in Basque and, as if she knew that what I was saying was not of the nicest quality, it made her furious. She was of the opinion, like my Mama, that I was possessed by some inner devil. I just thought English was an awful language and never cared if I learned it or not.

In spite of my aversion for her, I did admire the fact that she read us wonderful stories, and I listened carefully while she read to us about wonderful adventures and history and poetry, which I became interested in even while young.

I would sneak into the schoolroom and go through the stories just to see what the words looked like, and I would pretend to read.

Once I discovered books, what a wonderful world I opened up to myself. I found that I could read pretty well and could even converse with my brothers in that dumb language, although I never let Mrs. Brown know I could do it. She must have known, because I often found books left around that were my "size." After that, she was not near as harsh, and I think she left the ranch thinking I was not a completely hopeless creature.

As for me, I was so happy to be rid of Mrs. Brown and her awful dog Freckles. With the two of them, my bad nightmares came back. I still jump in alarm when I hear the words "Mississippi" or "Constantinople" because big words were her pride and joy. I must admit a certain admiration for her because she knew so much and carried it all in her big old cranky head.

That summer, I went to the sheep camp with Aita, accompanied by several of my favorite books. I loved them so much that I practically wore them out. I wonder how many times my poor dad listened to the children's stories as he drove his pickup down dusty camp roads.

Then he decided to teach me to read and write in our Basque language. It generally was not a written language, but is handed down to children from parents and grandparents.

I learned very quickly, as I had a prince of a teacher. I learned all the songs Dad would sing and laboriously wrote them all down in a little notebook while he corrected me in a much more pleasant way than that woman who still haunts me at times.

I spent a very happy care-free summer and I even tried to teach some of the herders to speak English. Most of them felt the same way I did about it though. They figured that they knew Basque, Spanish, and French and all the animals they were in contact with understood all three.

Aita was a man who loved to read. He loved his books even more than I did. He had the whole collection of the Zane Grey series, Erie Stanley Gardner, and Ellery Queen mysteries. He read the constitution, our history books, and quoted the preamble and the Gettysburg Address.

Where Aita was reading at every chance he got, Mama did not think much of books. In fact, books were something you picked up after the kids, dusted, and put back on the shelf.

She had not attended school in France beyond the third grade, but she had the most beautiful handwriting a person could wish for. It came from going to school and being taught by the nuns at the convent.

She did eventually learn to read and write English, but she never did learn to speak it very well. Nevertheless, she did awfully well in Basque and French. She still did not like to read and, if she did, she read aloud to everyone's irritation. We hated to be read the newspaper in an accented voice.

The next year, after Mrs. Brown, we got a wonderful and lovely teacher, Mrs. Peterson from Preston, Nevada. Her husband would bring her to our ranch on Mondays and come and get her every Friday night. She was pretty, gentle, wise, and taught with love and compassion, and all of us learned from her including Mama, with whom she had a special bond. She would set aside one to two hours a day when she would read aloud to us. We could not do our schoolwork fast enough for her to continue the current story. She taught us for two school years, after which she retired.

After Mrs. Peterson, we got Mrs. Boyd from Ibapah, Utah. She was much like our most recent teacher, preferring to teach in a gentle manner instead of the bullish ways of Mrs. Brown. She thought a willow stick was just for growing by a creek and was never cruel in her punishments. Her way was to take a messy essay, cross through it with a red pen, drop it in the waste basket, and make you do it all over again. Once or twice, she had to withhold the story she was reading to us and this worked very swiftly, for we did not want to miss *Swiss Family Robinson*, or *Treasure Island*, or even the Tarzan series.

Her Christmas gift to me one year was Louisa May Alcott's *Little Women*. How I loved that story and still do treasure it in my library. I had a special affinity for Jo and had a special place in my heart for Beth. We were introduced to history, adventure, and a little risqué language, such as in *The Grapes of Wrath*.

I was mesmerized by the wild adventures, the thrills, and the romance that I found in the world of books. I was lost in another world altogether. How many times did Mama send me to do some chore, only to find me buried in a book, my chores undone, having lost track of time? I always got a good slapping from her, got my book taken away, and had to do the chore anyway.

I started reading in bed until Mama yelled at me

to put out the light and go to sleep. Then, ingenious sinner that I was, I read under the covers with a flashlight until my little brother Pete told on me. If I ever got revenge on him, I would get another licking. Man, it was one round after another. No wonder Mama was strong and muscular; she got a lot of exercise punishing me.

At times, I would make faces at her turned back, but she always caught me. We had devised a way to make horrible smirky faces that meant you were supposed to turn blue and drop dead on the spot. It was an awful gesture involving lifting the lip in an ugly snarl and dropping one eye, and Mama hated it. Brother Pete was an expert at this gesture. He could do it perfectly with the side away from Mama so that she saw only his normal side and never suspected that her little angel was doing something bad. I should have been as lucky. I was always caught with my whole face hanging out.

John had such an innocent-looking face that Mama never suspected him anyway. Mike always got his revenge by yelling for his mother and she always came to his rescue at once. Arnaud had his own way of extracting revenge: he would pinch us under the arms in the fleshy part underneath, so we never made the face at him for reprisal was too swift and painful. Besides, he was getting too big to play such silly games anymore. He was already going to the sheep camp as the *torero*, or the herder in charge of the rams for the summer. He had his own camp and had to cook for himself. He had two of Queenie's pups to train and take care of and, though he was fourteen or so, he had all of the responsibility that the older herders had. He didn't have time for monkey business, and of course, he was our role model as we all looked up to him with respect and adoration. Boy, he really knew some neat stuff and shaved and everything.

He always knew the answers to the questions on my tongue
Always there to reassure me when I was scared and young
I could always count on him to protect me when I was little
He'd make me marvelous dolls and toys when he'd take time
to whittle.
Sometimes he'd make me cry and scream when he would
taunt and tease
And after scaring me half to death, he'd set my heart at ease
He was my cowboy hero, he was my buddy, brother
and my friend
I always counted on his love and the shoulder he would lend.
Sometimes he'd be so serious and would appear to be so grim
But he'd melt my heart nearly every time he gave
his crooked grin
He was a wonderful brother and he was surely
his father's son
And always was "tall in the saddle" when his
day's work was done

Like dad, he lost his earthly battles that he'd fought
one by one
He rode the horse called "death" into the setting sun
I miss him so, but I always feel him lingering
somewhere near
And very special memories come whispering in my ear!
I feel his pinches beneath my arms and he still pulls my hair
Sometimes the feeling he is near is more than I can bear
I know he's riding hard up there and he's got lots of
work to do
For now he rides those silvery hills and he's
Gods' special "buckaroo."

— In loving memory of my
beloved brother, Arnaud Santiago Paris

My world of books quickly opened up other worlds to me. I found the world of music and poetry, especially in the songs and poems that Aita recited to me. He was a natural poet, or *bertzolaria,* and this trait is very common to many of the Basques, perhaps because the language is musical and easy to rhyme.

It is tradition at Basque gatherings for poets to sing or rhyme at each other as a challenge. One will start his poem in rhyme and then cede his place to an opponent for an answer. This comes quickly, as they only have a few moments to think of an answer. This continues until one of the contestants cannot think of anything that is appropriate and he loses the contest.

This contest can go on for hours, and it always fascinated me. I tried to best my Dad a few times, but I never came close to it. We had some good laughs when I could only think of English words, and Aita would say "No, it has to be in Basque."

He was a very good singer, having a beautiful tenor voice that harmonized very well with Mama's. I remember going to the sheep camp in Aita's old truck and they would start to sing some of the old Basque songs that had ten or twenty verses. They knew them all by heart and Mama was very surprised when I could chime in and sing along with them. Then Aita would give me one of his poems and I had to go along with his "besting." I had to practice a lot, but I always enjoyed it very much. I still love old Basque songs.

Of all the herders and ranch hands we had, I think my very dearest friend was my Mama's brother Louis. He was so full of stories and fun and his nerves could never be frayed, no matter how much you tried. Very different from Mama except that they both shared a helacious temper, Otto Louis (*otto* means Uncle) had a good imagination and had time for all of us. He taught us many things, both good and bad, and would drop whatever he was doing to tell us a lot of stories. He taught us about Basque culture and all about his days in Eureka and Ely, and told us a lot of his hairy escapades.

One day, he came to tell us that he was going back to France. They were at war and his country needed him to go fight in the army.

Our other uncle, Francisco, was already in the war, and Louis figured that he was personally appointed to get rid of Hitler. Louis was going to slit Hitler's throat and rid the world of a bad smell. Then, he said, he was going to come back and herd sheep for the rest of his life. For a long time, he wrote us long letters and sent gifts from all the different places he served. We had them from Algeria, Italy, France, and South Africa. Then, there was nothing: no letters came, no gifts, no word!

Then came notification from Grandmama, who had gotten word from the French government, that both Goyhenetches had been taken prisoner and were being held in a camp in Germany somewhere.

Mama was especially concerned about Francisco, for he had never been strong in health, having suffered greatly at the hands of Uncle Cruz. We had heard a lot of starvation and deprivation and cruelty in the prison camps, and she feared for his life.

Deep in her heart, she just knew that Otto Louis could hold his own in a lot of situations and could probably find a way out if there was one possible. She figured he could knock the "hell" out of any German prison guard.

During all this time that her brothers were prisoners, I never once saw her cry. I suppose that her strict and tearless upbringing still prevailed. It went against her grain to let anyone see her grief. I suppose that when no one was looking, there must have been tears shed.

I missed my Otto Louis so much and wanted him back. I let her know of my woes quite often. This constituted a few slaps to keep me quiet.

Then one day, there was a letter from France from my dear uncle. He had escaped along with three other Basque boys and made his way back to France.

Uncle Francisco remained a prisoner of war until the end of the war when he was liberated. He returned to France to live a life of semi-invalidism with no care and little food, he never quite recovered from it. He had contracted consumption.

Louis came back to herd sheep, but those wonderful and laughing black eyes never smiled again. Now, his stories were bitter and sad, and yes, I did see Mama cry when she met him. He picked her up, swung her around, and pulled her hair, but something was missing. Otto Louis was not the same carefree man that he had been when he went to kill Hitler.

He took his donkey and his dog and took to the hills to care for the sheep, and we did not see him often after that. He became a semi-recluse and took to heavy drinking. It got a bit better after a few years and he became a little less reclusive, but the drinking kept up and, in a short time, he decided to go back to France to live. He made several trips back to the United States, the last one when my son Mike was small. Uncle Louis doted on my son who could wrap him around his little finger. He was a devoted babysitter and my little boy loved him as much as I did.

When he returned to France, unable to settle down anywhere, we saw him off with heavy hearts and never saw him again. He apparently died when he had been heavily drinking and attempted to cross the river in Banca. He had never learned to swim, fell into the river, and drowned.

Our Grandmama died a few years before Louis. She had been cooking at the open fire in their house, hit her foot on the threshold, and fell into the open fire. She was alone at the time and it was a long period before Francisco found her. She had been fatally burned. She was eighty-six at the time of her death.

He came back to the arms of his family fold,
at first appearing to be the Louis of old –
but there was something missing.
He was back from the war,
but was a changed man
changed in a way that only war can –
there was something missing.
In fighting a war, there's something that dies
and my uncles' smile did not reach his eyes –
there was something missing
The peace he had sought, he never could find

the war in his country still preyed on his mind –
there was something missing.
Tormented by memories, he started to drink wine,
dulling pain and ability to think –
there was something missing!
He went back to France where soon after he died.
I miss his fun and his great Basque pride –
for now Otto Louis is missing!

Mama was a wonderful cook who never used packages or mixes or prepared foods, except for her inevitable oatmeal. She also never used recipes! I used to watch her cook and, as I tried to learn how, I used to try to write down some sort of recipe, but it was impossible because she never measured anything. It was a scoop of this, a dab of that, a pinch of something else, a couple of "dibbles," or paloops of another. I would finally give up in desperation and would have to use my own judgment on measuring. I do the same thing now and when I find a recipe I like, always thinking I can improve on it, my garbage disposal eats a lot of failures. We had the four-legged kind at the ranch. They were called pigs.

I will never forget the first time she tried a Betty Crocker packaged cake mix. She rolled her eyes and clacked her tongue and never in a lifetime would she believe that this box of yellow flour could be turned into a cake.

Imagine her surprise when the beautiful cake

came out of the oven. Of course, we made homemade frosting, but still the cake did not hold a candle to her scratch cakes.

Then sadly, she discovered an instant pudding packaged mix called Amazo. You just put it in a bowl, added milk, and beat it until it thickened. It was a time saver for her, but such a disappointment for me and Aita. Now, we only got her lovely tapioca pudding from scratch on Sundays. The rest of the time, it was stinking old cardboard-y tasting Amazo. If Amazo was on our grocery list, we both forgot it.

She often took leftovers and turned them into new and exciting dishes to tickle the palates of the many guests and family members that always seemed to crowd her table. It seemed like every time we had company, they lingered at the house until eating time, knowing they would be asked to stay and enjoy one of her gastronomical delights. Her table at Easter, Thanksgiving, and Christmas groaned with sheer delight.

I like to blame her for every ugly pound I have put on my frame, for with the exception of oatmeal and good old Amazo, I have never found a food I do not like.

These foods still cling to me so lovingly and heavily that I think it was Mama's legacy to show how much she did love us: a fat stuffed kid was a fat stuffed happy kid.

Mama was an incessantly, tireless housekeeper, an avid gardener, and poultry farmer. She kept our family fed, our big house immaculately clean, and the orchard well-tended. She preserved all the vegetables and fruits we needed for winter survival, not only for family use but for the sheep camp provisions. She canned everything. We did not have freezers or refrigeration, except for the cold box, and all things had to be canned or dried. Her dried apple or peach pies were something to die for. Oh, wonderful aromas came from her ovens.

She raised chickens, ducks, geese, and infernal turkeys. We would have to boil chicken eggs and crumble them into small pieces to feed the baby turkeys. Then the greedy little monsters would "guawp" and choke and stagger around the pen with their beaks wide open until some of them would actually collapse. We'd have to massage their throats until the feed would find its way into their craws. If it rained, you had to rush out and get them into shelter because Mama was told that a drop of rain on a new turkey would kill it if it landed on its head; I think someone fed her a big bunch of turkey melarkey. I hated trying to round up so many baby turkeys, with their mamas flying around trying to peck my eye balls out, and I wondered how wild turkeys survived without someone to help them and feed them boiled eggs. Who massaged them when they "guawped" and choked?

Once my brother John, then a toddler, followed

me into the turkey pen and, thinking the babies were mamutzac, or bugs, started smashing them with his feet. He killed a few of them before I could stop him, and I got the whipping for it. Stupid turkeys, always caused me no end of grief. The only place I had any use for them was on the table at Thanksgiving, stuffed with Mama's delicious stuffing and baked golden brown in the oven.

We collected down from the geese and ducks, and Mama made pillows and comforters. The herders liked her down comforters because they were warm and easy to transport. We usually kept the wool comforters she made, for they were too heavy for the camps, especially if they got wet. They were very welcome on a cold winter night though. If someone perspired at night, the wool would get a little rank smelling. My little brother often wet the bed at night and would wake in the morning smelling very "sheepy."

The other animals on the ranch that I could not stand were the pigs. We always raised twenty or so pigs depending on the size of the litters, and Mama would make sausages or chorizos, bacons and hams, and *murcillas*, or blood sausages. They were delicious and very rich (cholesterol city), but we did not worry about that in those days; I had never heard of cholesterol in my youth.

Mama made salt pork and side ribs, head cheese, and lomos, which was the loin of the animal cut into chunks and cooked and put in preserve in rendered lard for summer use when there was no fresh meat.

I had to help my brothers in slopping the hogs and how I despised that job. They were very dirty, smelled terrible, and got right in the trough eating around each other's feet. Such a racket you never heard.

All my brothers had to do to start a fight was to call me a pig. Them's fightin words all my life. I would take to them with anything I could find to hit them with, including a pitch fork at one time. Mama would have to haul me off, literally by the hair, and force me, yelling and screaming, into the house.

Pete was especially bad because he never let up on me. He'd call me pig, make his "bad face," and get away with it. I'd generally catch him in the barn later and beat the crud out of him.

Every year, around November or early December, we would have the *matanza,* or butchering. Aita would shoot the pigs in the head, hoist them up quickly, and slit their throats, catching the blood in a bucket. It was my job to stir the blood until it was cool because it could not be allowed to clot for the *murcillas*. Then the carcasses were dropped into very hot water and all the hair was scraped off. The smell of the blood and the heating fire would make me choke and retch and many times I almost puked in the bucket of blood.

This memory still gags me and I attribute this chore to the fact that I cannot stand barbequed or grilled smoked-meat. I always think of "pig blood and pig fire."

Mama would cut off all the skin after she rendered the fat and make cracklings that were such a looked for treat.

We also had to clean miles and miles of intestines to make casings for the chorizos. They had to be cleaned in very cold water so we would sit by the creek and clean and scrape until our hands were nearly frozen. Oh that awful cold and that terrible smell. When everything was on the table, I would soon forget all my aversions. Nothing went to waste, except the hair and the oink. The boys even blew up the pig bladders and made good strong footballs. I would crack the knuckle bones off the pigs feet, after Mama cooked them in a delicious chili sauce, to make playing jacks.

Next to turkeys, the pigs were very low on the pecking order, as far as I was concerned. I just hope if there is reincarnation, I don't come back as a pig or a turkey.

Life on the ranch was quite wonderful and though we all had our responsibilities and chores, we had fun growing up. I missed sheep camp life and was ready to go whenever Aita made camps and checked his herds. I especially loved the time the herds left the summer camps in the high Ruby Mountains in Elko to be trailed to the White River range where our ranch was located and where they wintered on the flats.

In the summer, I often went fishing at Soldier Creek where the big camp was. Aita would tie a string on a length of willow and, while he did all the fishing, I actually thought that I could catch fish with no hook. Of course, he caught all the fish, but I always had such a good time just being with him. Plus, he always caught enough for both of us anyway. He always had a gunnysack full and never abided by fishing limits.

Mama would be glad to see us coming back safely and all in good health, for she was expecting us to have an accident or get bitten by a snake because Soldier Creek was a haven for rattlesnakes. I never worried about anything bad when I was with Dad. Walking home, hand-in-hand, listening to him sing, or making up verses, my world was perfect and nothing bad ever loomed on my horizon.

Back at home, tired, dirty, and with a case of bad hair, it was off with the overalls, into a tub of hot water, a stiff hairbrush, and – if I protested while she tried to scrub my skin off – a swift slap with the hair brush.

My fairytale world would soon vanish, though I must say, I went out of my way to irritate Mama. I probably did deserve every slap that came my way or was administered on my bare backside as I yelled and hollered all the while she was scrubbing the grit off me. She thought I had a tireless pair of lungs and a tongue that reached down to my toes. In all these shenanigans though, it seemed there were never any tears shed. But as far as noise was concerned, I made plenty. I knew that while she was scraping and pulling all my hair out, that I had her full attention all to myself. I must have not minded it too much because I never did learn to keep my big yelling mouth shut.

Soldier Creek, Ruby Mountains, Nevada

Arnaud Paris

A Day with Aita

Sitting on the bank with a pole
at Soldier Creek
Watching the fish in the hole
darting silvery and quick
In my hand a hookless willow stick
tied up with some twine
I was fishing with my dad and the whole
wide world was mine.
He'd break into happy laughter,
he'd tell stories or he'd sing
I loved fishing with my dad and the
happy times he'd bring.
Too soon, the setting sun would give
its last rays of the day
We'd gather up our fishing gear
and head off along our way.
Those summer days were perfect
and the best times I ever had
Were sitting on the creek bank
and fishing with my dad
I knew the day would end soon
and maybe mama would be mad
But what a way to spend the day,
just fishing with my dad!

Sign for the Paris Ranch

Aerial view of the Pleasant Valley Ranch

A whole day on the road in a big old truck filled
with all our possessions
Four cranky kids, a mean old dog, and a lot of
dreams and obsessions
We rounded a curve around a little hill and came
to a tall wooden gate
We could hardly see what lay beyond
for the journey had ended quite late
This tiresome move that was breaking
our hearts had started so early that day
And the look of relief on my fathers' face
told me that life was okay!
The meadows were dotted with horses and
cows and the few sheep kept by dad
His eyes showed pride and a sadness
there for the dream ranch he'd always had
Mama's critical eyes were looking
about but she couldn't find fault with this
She gave her approval to the man at her side
with a soft and gentle kiss
At the sight of the house and the orchard below,
my heart lifted from its depression
That we'd love this place and be happy here,
was my first, startled impression
I felt his pride and felt great love as dad gave
me a lopsided grin
But I saw tears in his eyes, as he opened the door
and led his family in.

Pleasant Valley Ranch

Pleasant Valley Ranch

"The new ranch was big and beautiful and we had many of the new things we had never had at the old place."

THE NEW RANCH

Aita decided that, with the demands of his large family, he needed a bigger ranch. He purchased the Stewart Polkinghorne Ranch in Pleasant Valley, near Winnemucca, Nevada and sold our Forest Home. We moved north and west across Nevada.

Now, the boys were all happy because they loved cattle and were cowboys at heart but I remained a sheepherder. I found out that Aita had sold his sheep herds to buy his sons a cattle ranch and I was very resentful. I hated cows and big rough, long-horned bulls scared me out of my wits.

The trip from Ely was a long, dusty, and for the most part quite silent with each of us lost in our own thoughts. I looked over at Mama and saw rare tears in her eyes as she sat on the seat of our big heavily loaded ranch truck with brother Pete clenched in her arms.

Her tears frightened me and I felt the torture of my world being changed as I lost another part of my life.

The new ranch was big and beautiful and we had many of the new things we had never had at the old place. The house had a bathroom, which replaced "Ye Olde Outhouse," and we had a freezer, a refrigerator, and electricity. At Forest Home, we had had a "meat house," which consisted of a crude shed hung with burlap sacks and screening. We'd kept the eggs, meats, and perishables cold by keeping the "gunny sacks" wet and letting the wind blow through. We'd used kerosene lamps and wax candles for lighting and it had been my job to keep the darn chimneys clean, so electricity was welcome, for it had none of those to keep clean.

In spite of having all modern conveniences, Mama worked harder than ever, grew a bigger garden, made more butter and cheese, preserved more groceries and meats than ever before, and each of us had more chores to do even though we had a more convenient way of doing them.

Since Mama grew most of our "living," we would make a trip to town about every three months to buy sugar, coffee, flour, oil, (of course) oatmeal, and medications. Everything else, practically, was homegrown. I loved these outings, but still was always glad to get home. We bought Amazo too.

We always got one quarter apiece when we went to town because we never had allowances. It was pretty easy to put one's hand in Dad's pocket and always find a dime or a nickel with a finger on his lips to keep it a secret. It soon got to the point that we could not buy as much candy as a few years back when we got ten pieces of candy for just one penny. The boys always blew their quarter on big Hersheys bars and would run out of "stuff" long before the next outing.

Once I conned my two younger brothers out of their two quarters and blew the whole wad on a book! It was *Black Beauty* and what a treasure I had. I figured it was well worth the brotherly "punch out" I received when they saw the little meager sack of candy I bought with left over pennies.

Despite their disappointment, they loved the story almost as much as I did. I had to give up my quarters for the next five or six times, but I always had left overs.

We always saved the last piece of chewing gum for days and days, taking turns chewing it long after the flavor was gone. The bad thing was that whoever chewed it last would keep the wad on the back of the head board at night. We had to beat Mama to it in the morning because if she found it we got a sharp slap, got called little pigs, and she'd throw it out. We mourned that luscious piece of gum that looked up at us so forlornly from the bottom of the coal bin many times.

Mama was a firm believer in oatmeal and cod liver oil. All five of us would line up early in the morning and, holding our noses, would swallow that evil-smelling concoction that was guaranteed to keep us alive and healthy. Sure, if that stuff didn't kill you on the spot, you would live for a long time. Then it was off to the table for a very large pot of oatmeal, which tasted strangely like the cod-liver oil. This oatmeal was only during the school year, for in the summer time it was eggs, pancakes, sausage, bacon, and the whole bit. Mama figured oatmeal was brain food.

She bought the large boxes of Mothers Oats that had dishes in them. The large size had plates (dinner ones), and the small size had cups and saucers. Needless to say, we had a lot of dinner plates. I sure envied Aita, who looked to be pretty healthy and was not forced to eat "horse food."

I think there was only one food that Mama could not stand. That was hominy. She never would serve it, but I would eat it gladly whenever I went to someone's house who served it.

One thing Aita and I missed when he sold his sheep was Dutch oven "mountain oysters." These tidbits were cooked slowly in oil with plenty of garlic in the Dutch oven over low heat. Whenever we docked the lambs (cut their tails off), the testicles were removed from the male lambs, washed very carefully, soaked in vinegar and water all night after all the cords were removed one by one, and cooked in this way. They were an awful lot of labor, to prepare but they sure made up for it in flavor. We always had a lot of help during the docking because people would come in bunches to "help" us so they could get a shot at mountain oysters. Of course, there were thousands of them, but all the guests at the table made short work of them. Mama cooked the tails also, but there was nothing to eat on them. In the same way as the oysters, they were cooked in dutch oven, but you had to eat a million to make a meal.

I remember my first taste of calf "oysters." I was very disappointed because even though we cooked them the same way, they tasted "cowey." I didn't care for the taste of beef, so I always waited for when we butchered a lamb or wether.

We had spring lamb every Easter and my brothers, who insisted they hated the smell of sheep (typical cowmen), did more than their share to the golden brown roasted leg of lamb or good old fried lamb chops. I guess the cooked lamb didn't smell too bad for their exalted palates.

When we still had sheep, Aita would tell me that sheep are very silly creatures. They would reject their lambs for no sane reason and I was told not to handle the newborns at all. If the mother ewe smelled anything but herself on the lamb, she would walk away from it. I found myself often playing with some of the prettiest ones, and of course, the ewe would reject it. So it happened that I had a lot of abandoned babies.

We called these bummer lambs leppies, and sometimes, if the herder had time, the abandoned lambs wore the skin of a dead lamb and the bereaved mother would accept the lamb as her own. Sometimes the lamb would be put into a small pen with the ewe and she'd be forced to nurse the lamb until her milk passed through it and she would take it back. Most of the time, with thirteen thousand head of sheep, it was not possible to take the time, and the lambs died. So I had a lot of baby lambs that I fed from a bottle. When they were big enough to survive on grass, they were taken to the herds and put in with the others. Not knowing they were sheep, they would follow the herder and his dogs and most of the herders did not like them. They disrupted sheep camp life terribly. My favorite herder, Fernando, always took my lambs and did not seem to mind when they followed him everywhere. Poor dear Fernando, "keeper of the lambs;" he looked like my idea of the "Good Shepherd."

I told Aita I was going to marry Fernando, but there were about forty years difference in our lives. I said we would own a sheep ranch and all the dreams of a small child would come true. Instead, when I got old enough, I married Louis his nephew, who was the son of his sister in France. I kept Fernando in the family and in my heart, but I never did get my sheep ranch.

Mama was forever worried about ticks. Being around so many lambs, I picked them up all the time and once even had a sheep dip bath. The ticks fell off, but so did a lot of skin. I have been ever grateful that she was not mad at me that day, or she would have used the undiluted dip and I would still be trying to grow hair.

We did lose a herder, Fermin Urrutia, to Rocky Mountain fever, which is carried by ticks. He was a sweet and gentle man who had married in France and left his wife there expecting a baby. He never saw the child he adored except in pictures his wife sent him occasionally. She had no wish to leave her family for the uncertainty of the states, so Fermin made up his mind to go to France and bring her and the child back with him. Before he could bring his plans to fruition, he died from tick fever.

There are many aspen trees carved by Fermin with the name of his daughter, Anna Marie and the date of birth. He was a special friend of both Mama and Aita from the old country and had lived with us for about six years when we lost him.

All the herders loved Mama. She took the place of the mother so many of the young men had left in the old country. She was their friend and sometimes their doctor.

I often saw her administering to cuts, wounds, bad colds, tick bites, broken hearts, and even helping with such things as hangovers. What her mustard plasters and poultices could not cure, her chicken soup would.

I don't recall any of us ever going to a doctor, except Mike who got pneumonia and had to be hospitalized. Other than the normal childhood diseases, we never got sick, so there was a thing or two to be said for cod liver oil and oatmeal.

All of our hired hands were treated like members of the family. Except for the herders, who were out in the hills, the hands ate at our family table and had their clothes done along with the family's. Mama even catered to their likes and dislikes in special dishes and desserts. If any of them went to town, they always brought her some small gift back, even Frijolito, who squandered all his money every time he went to town. He would always get Mama a gift first, before he I began his drinking spree, for his cash was soon gone on the gambling and whiskey and women who frequented his life.

In the autumn, when the sheep were trailed down toward the ranch, the herders would come for Thanksgiving, and again for Christmas, for the big feasts that we held. Of course, the fete would go on until early morning and then each sick man came around for a big plate of *bahachuri* sopa, or garlic soup, which was known to cure hangovers.

Each year at Christmas, every herder was given a present of two pairs of Levis or overalls, two shirts, four pairs of socks (although some never wore socks, preferring to wrap their feet in gunny sacks), two pairs of shoes, and a hand-knit sweater that Mama made during the course of the year. I think Mama's way of relaxing was to sit at night and knit or crochet. We had crocheted table cloths, bedspreads, and doilies all over the house. Each of us had embroidered pillow cases over homemade pillows on our beds. No matter how pretty the cases were, the pillows still smelled like chickens because they were made from soft chicken feathers from the hens we butchered on weekends. We had a fine chicken dinner every Sunday and spent a lot of time cleaning the feathers.

I only saw Mama's monumental temper directed at one of the herders or ranch hands once in my lifetime.

She had sent me to gather eggs, which was a job that I utterly detested. I had found one of the wily hens that had hidden her eggs in the barn and I was busy at the job of pulling them out with a stick from under the manger. They would have to be kept separate from the other eggs and would have to be candled for freshness. I heard some sort of a commotion behind me and, before I could get up, was engulfed from behind by two arms that had such strength in them that it sent terror to my heart. He turned me around and started to tear off my new shirt that Mama had made for me, while exposing himself. He had almost succeeded in tearing off the shirt when, blindly and entirely by instinct, I kicked as hard as I could and then watched in terror as he fell to his knees in pain.

In absolute fright, I saw by his eyes that if I did not escape him now he would probably kill me when he regained himself. I ran for the house, shaky and sick to my stomach at having to explain my torn shirt to Mama. I blurted out what had happened and prepared myself for a beating for the shirt and, as I looked down and saw that my shoes covered by egg yolks, another one for all those eggs I'd broke.

Her reaction scared me silly, for she hugged me and kissed me, asking worriedly if he had hurt me. I was so surprised by her actions that I didn't know if I should stay or run.

She ran for the barn with her big "pig sticker" knife but could not find the man. If she had, she would have run the knife into his heart and fed his body to the pigs.

Aita, of course, found the man and, though he was a gentle man and was awfully careful not to lose his temper because he could turn violent, beat the ranch hand within an inch of his life and sent him on his way afoot. I don't know how the man got to Winnemucca because we lived more than fifty miles from town and he had not been in the best of all conditions to walk that distance.

A few years after that, we heard that the man had been sent to the penitentiary in Carson City for molesting the seven-year-old son of a ranchhand on a farm where he had found a job after his fiasco at our ranch.

I wished I had told my parents about the many times he pinched me or tried to touch me. I might have saved myself a lot of misery and probably that other child as well, but I was a very naive eleven year old.

Once Mama and Aita had gone to Elko for the funeral of one of her cousins and, while attending the funeral, she suffered a kidney stone. She had to be hospitalized, so they hired this man to cook for the riding crew and the rest of the family.

He came into my bedroom one morning, after the cowboys had left, and pulled off all the covers just to wake me up. When he heard the outer gate slam, for one of the cowboys was running late and stopped by for a cup of coffee, the man ran from my room. I was lucky the cowboy was late that morning.

My newfound closeness with Mama did not last very long. Soon after that I asked her some kind of question about a friend of hers who was expecting a baby, and she knocked me on my rear end for being a snot. So much for my sex education.

She still had her temper and most of it was unleashed on me. Our Dad did not take too much of it. He would stand it just so long, then walk away telling her to tie a knot in her long, lean tongue. When he returned, things would be on an even keel again and they would be whirling around the kitchen humming a tune. What a pair: one so kind and gentle, the other so severe and volatile. I guess it is true that opposites attract, because they always appeared to us to be a perfectly matched couple. Now, I can step back and see who worked the hardest at the marriage.

Mama's cross was the famous temper that Uncle Cruz had never succeeded in beating out of her. I wonder why she could never see the priest in herself nor recognize the essence of herself in me.

Often I have bitten my tongue, or stopped my hand from reacting because I have looked in a mirror and seen the same thing that was in Mama Marie.

At the new ranch, everything seemed to be going very well. Things were good in the cattle business and the boys were happy. Mama was happy, but Aita and I still missed the sheep. My brothers would laugh and say they were glad to be rid of the "stink of sheep."

We had a school at the ranch and had a very wonderful teacher, Mrs. Bradley from Utah, who lived at the ranch with us during the school terms. The first year was fine and we learned a lot because Mrs. Bradley had a lot of time for individual attention and she had a lot of knowledge to impart, as she had been extensively traveled.

We advanced two grades that year, except for Mike who didn't want to go to school and did not apply a bit of himself. He found himself in the same grade

I was in and this was right up his alley. Now he could copy all my work because we sat at the same table.

During the second year, Mrs. Bradley would give us our lessons, then drop off to sleep and we would quickly run out to play. We would make it back to school before she woke up, but I guess Mama wondered why we had so many recesses. She caught us playing rodeo in the corral and we all got a good spanking. She found Mrs. Bradley at her desk, fast asleep, and the good woman found herself on the end of Mama's rapid tongue. None of us knew then that she suffered from some sort of illness. When she went home at Christmas vacation, Mrs. Bradley fell asleep and never woke up again.

Mama blamed herself because she figured she ought to have noticed the woman was ill when she fell asleep at the table a few times. It's a wonder she didn't dose the poor old lady with cod liver oil and oatmeal. It certainly was a great loss for all of us. She was a good person and a fine friend to all the family. Mama had been taking some lessons from her in reading and writing in English, but did not practice much after Mrs. Bradley's demise.

"Otto Louis had a good imagination and had time for all of us. He taught us many things, both good and bad and would drop whatever he was doing to tell us a lot of stories."

THE MOVE TO TOWN

We stayed at the ranch for the duration of the school year and, in September, my parents purchased a home and we went to live in Winnemucca.

On the day we were to move to town, Mike threw his big bed roll on his horse and disappeared into the hills for a few days. He wasn't about to move to town and go to school. He thought he had enough schooling to cowboy for a living, so he ended his formal education; he had not finished seventh grade.

Arnaud elected not to finish high school, so John, Pete, and I, the three musketeers, moved to town, hating every darn minute of it. We were the original "hicks from the sticks," and thought we had already learned what there was to know.

We quickly found that school in town was very different from the ranch. There were so many more kids in our classes, many more teachers, and nobody read the stories we loved anymore. We were a rather sad group of ranch kids who went to the ranch on weekends only now.

How wonderful it was to return to the ranch each weekend and crowd all our activities in to two days. We all hated town life, but Mama hated it most of all of us. She stuck it out for a while, but then she went back to the ranch, leaving me to watch the boys and take care of the big old house, which I had to keep waxed and polished like glass all the time. The boys were not any trouble for me because I was used to taking care of them anyway. Every once in a while, they would rebel on me and I had to exert my authority to keep them in line.

John could be managed sensibly, but young Pete was more of a handful and could be very rebellious and stubborn. I often "talked to him with my hands," and sometimes he would talk back when he was about to be subdued by a sister.

We had a lot of fun when Mama was not around to censor our lives. We would walk around uptown and window shop, for we seldom had money to spend, and we never once had oatmeal for breakfast.

Mama would surprise us with a visit once in a while and the house would never be pristine enough for her. With school and boys to take care of, the housework slipped. No matter how many hours I spent on it, the house always looked lived in when she visited. She never came when it smelled like soap and Pine Sol, but when it smelled like dirty socks and wet towels, we were sure to get surprised. I never dared to let the house get filthy, but it sure looked used sometimes.

My Mama was always an apostle of cleanliness. Even the bunkhouse had to be swept every day and the beds made as they were in the house. Once you made the bed, it was a sin to sit on it again because if you messed it up you had to make it again. Every wash day, the clothes were washed and ironed; even the towels and socks underwent the pressure of the flat irons.

Her favorite saying was to wear clean underwear every day because you never knew when you might get sick or hurt and have to go to the doctor or hospital.

Once, I fell out of an apple tree while picking apples and Mama made me change my underclothes before I could go to the hospital. There I was with a "greenstick fracture" of the ankle, fifty-two miles from the hospital, nearly in a faint from pain, changing my underpants.

Aita had been beside himself, for none of us had ever been hurt before and he could see it was bad, but there was my Mama standing over me making me change my clothes. That was Mama.

Life went along at a very merry pace and everyone was so happy. The ranch was thriving and the boys were happy with their cows and horses. They were accomplished and deft cowboys now and gave no more thought to the sheep that had made this all possible, except for the lamb chops on the table or the succulent leg of lamb with roasted potatoes.

I missed the herds very much and I'm sure Aita did too. I could often be found in the meadow with the few that we kept around the ranch for meat, playing with the new baby lambs that were born each spring.

Often when there was work for me to do, especially in the hog-butchering season, I would open the gate to the field where the sheep grazed, and take them to the hills in back of the ranch, where they grazed on new grass and where I watched the lambs gamboling and trying to out jump each other. I often thought of quitting school and talking Aita into buying more sheep so I could be his herder. I would go to the hills with my sheep and dogs and live the hermitic life of the herder in complete happiness. I could read to my heart's content, and never have to do anything else but look after my beloved sheep and be with my wonderful dog. Of course, I never gave a thought to all the work sheepherding could be.

Mama would not be around to give me the dickens all the time and I could let the dogs lick my few dishes clean so I wouldn't have to wash them. I could leave my bedroll in the same condition every day. I would never have to sweep the floor or do anything that looked like work. I was basically a very indolent person at heart.

Then suddenly, Aita started feeling sick. He was tired all the time and had very little appetite. He had a lot of blood in his urine and back aches constantly, so a quick conference with our doctor and he was sent to Oakland, California to a specialist who diagnosed him with cancer of the bladder. Then there began to be many trips to Oakland for radiation treatments. I went with him on the train for many of these trips, for he would be so helpless and weak after these treatments

Aita

he had to be kept in bed at least a week. This was no small feat, for Aita had always been so strong and active that keeping to his bed was all a waste of time. He hated every minute of the treatments until finally they were terminated and he was then pronounced cancer free! What good news that was, for he very quickly gained back all the weight he had lost and looked like the Aita of old.

Things went along well for the next five years, but then came more bad news. The cancer was back, but this time it was in his colon. It quickly spread to other parts of his body and he lost both buttocks to large tumors. He underwent seventeen operations to try and conquer his disease and I stayed with him in San Francisco where he was practically a guinea pig in cancer research because the doctors did not know much about it in those days. They literally cut him to pieces until they decided that there was nothing else to do for him but put him on pain relievers and send him home to die. They cut him a colostomy, which he hated, and he soon lost the will to fight. Mama would dress his dreadful wounds with tenderness and cleaned his colostomy bag every few hours, sleeping in a chair near his bed at night, holding his hand, for he suffered such great pain that he could not sleep even with morphine-induced relief. We could hear him moaning in pain throughout the long nights. He was unable to eat, though Mama tempted him with all his favorite foods, and was literally starving to death. The little bit of Ensure he was able to hold down was barely keeping him alive.

Into this world of pain and sorrow and hopeless disease came my godmother, Maria Echevarria, to assist Mama in taking care of Aita. She did the cooking, heavy work, and the great job of comforting that she was so capable of doing.

I turned to her wonderful arms in my sorrow and loneliness and I was not turned away, no matter how busy she was. I never felt like I had Mama, and now I was losing my beloved Aita. I had my "Amatchi." She was a wonderful person, so very understanding, kind and gentle to Aita, and such a beautiful friend and comforter to me. God bless her soul and keep a special place for me at her side if I am ever lucky enough to get to Heaven. They say that God has plans for every soul he sends to Earth and her plans were to be there for me.

One afternoon, I was sitting near Aita's bed to give my Mama a rest, holding his hand and wiping his face gently with a soft cloth, for he even had bed sores on his face, when he grabbed my arm hard and tried to speak. I knew something was very wrong and I held his hand tightly and kissed him gently. He died with the lopsided smile on his face that I had loved so well. "Get Mama" were the last words he uttered.

My heart was shattered and I thought it would

never mend. My beautiful, gentle Aita was gone from me on his eternal trip and I could never be with him again. In my agony, I pushed Mama further away from me and never stopped to think she might have been suffering also. At any rate, the chasm widened between us and I drew further into my shell. If it had not been for my brother Arnaud, I don't think I would ever have come out of it. He helped me a lot by literally stepping into Aita's shoes and becoming the father figure in our lives. He was strong and had a lot of faith and he never let us down.

Matters between Mama and myself disintegrated quickly, for in less than two years she had remarried and moved to another state. Of course, I was lost, bitter, and felt so very betrayed. I was angry and very resentful of her and my stepfather. How could she stop loving Dad so soon? I never did stop to think that perhaps she had been lonely and lost and still craved love and companionship, for she was only in her early forties at the time. I should have felt how devastated she was by his death, for I know how much they did love each other. I have only good and loving memories of my mom and dad together. I know that the love and relationship remained untouched, even by another marriage and the birth of my little sister, Josephine. I can see now that the marriage was another part of her life and had nothing to do with her past love and life. I still felt a great resentment and there was no getting past it, for I still feel a great deal of it.

We were eventually reconciled, but there remained always, a little wall, a little pushing away, and the wall remained firmly entrenched in old feelings and hurts.

Mama never knew how much she wounded me when she refused to attend my wedding. I will never understand or forgive that last blow she dealt me on what was the happiest day of my life.

I know I had Aita's blessing, for I saw him at the ceremony for just an instant, even if it was in my imagination. Once again, I saw the flashing blue eyes and the crooked smile I so loved when he was with us. I also saw a sadness and shadow that I knew Mama's absence had put there, for I recalled seeing that same sadness there many times when I was a child. It cut to the very heart of me.

The years went by and Mama remained the same obstinate strong-willed "woman with attitude" she had always been. She raised her second daughter with more leniency and my sister Josie perhaps has a different side to her relationship. It has been hard for me to write this story without letting my resentment and personal grudges show. I do apologize to my other siblings if this story tarnishes the memory of Mama. I am speaking only of my own feelings for her. If it is possible to love a person and dislike them at the same time, then that was how it was with me.

When she passed away from diabetic complications, I gazed upon her peaceful face and I wanted to tell her how much I loved her and always had. Strangely enough, she now looked very much at peace and her face resembled the way it had looked at night when I was a child. It was soft and reposed and her severe look was gone.

How very much I wanted to whisper "I love you." Instead, with a peaceful heart, I whispered: "goodbye my mama Marie."

Marie's grandchildren Mary Ann Paris and Bert Paris, playing on ice, Pleasant Valley Ranch

Left to right: Marie Jeanne Paris Etcheverry, Arnaud Paris, Alice Paris, Mike Paris, Louis Errea, Joan Marie Paris Errea, John Paris, Pete Paris, and Yvonne Paris

Marie Jeanne Paris Etcheverry

EPILOGUE

Mama was remarried in 1953 to Juan Etcheverry of Yuba City, California and they had another daughter, Josephine. My sister had, I believe, a much closer relationship than the one I had. Mama was never demonstrative with her but Josie, being very much more "vocal" than I was, stood up for her rights and did not suffer the recriminations of my life. Josie has never been one to repress her feelings and sometimes lets them out with a bang. I wish I had done that so many times. Josie is very happily married to Meliton Irigoyen of Spain, and they have two beautiful children, Christina and Francisco.

My oldest brother, Arnaud, was married to Alice Gallio from a neighboring ranch in Unionville. They had two children: Maryann, who is married to Lynn Hammond of Golconda, Nevada, has a beautiful daughter, Lisa Marie; and Bert, his son, is married to Jill Filipini, who is from a Battle Mountain, Nevada ranching family, and they have two delightful sons, Martin and Michael.

Arnaud passed away in 1984 from the same dreaded disease that took Aita in almost identical conditions. Once again, I lost my rock and guidance and it has been very hard to manage without him. His widow, Alice, remarried Raymond Norcutt, a family friend, who is a wonderful caring man who has become a dear part of our family.

John and Mike never married, but sold the family ranch and moved to Lovelock, Nevada, where Mike retired and John is employed by the Pershing County road department.

Youngest brother, Pete, married Yvonne Giurlani and had two children, John and Stephanie. John is not yet married and Stephanie is married to Steven Swan. So far no children, but I'm sure Pete will treasure any grandchildren that come his way.

Pete pursued a career with a large utility company and became a vice president. He is truly the VP of our family.

I married Louis Errea of Baigorri, France, who came to this country at a very young age to herd sheep. He tired very soon of herding and pursued a career at the Nevada State Department of Transportation until his retirement.

We have two very well-loved children, Mike and Lianne. Mike is not yet married and is pursuing a career with the State of Nevada, taking his Dad's place when Louis retired. Lianne is married to a local attorney, John Iroz, who was also the product of immigrant parents. They have, so far, one child, my one and only grandson, Martin. They operate their own office where John, my beloved son-in-law, practices law.

My two children were raised in a strict home, where they were expected to grow into responsible, caring adults and have done so admirably. They were disciplined, sometimes very stringently, but always with love. Always with great love. I never tire of showing them that I love them.

The author with family.
Standing: Pete Paris, Mike Errea, John Paris,
Mary Ann Hammond, Martin Iroz,
Stephanie Swan, Lianne Iroz, Scott Swan,
Lisa Cassinelli, Kelley Paris, Jack Paris, Katie Cassinelli
Seated: John Paris and Joan Errea

MY MAMA MARIE'S BASQUE RECIPES

Mama's Vegetable Soup

1 small head cabbage
4 large carrots
2 large leeks
2 stalks celery
1 small onion
2 large potatoes
1 pound fresh green beans (or one can cut green beans)
2 fresh tomatoes (skinned)
2 cloves of garlic, diced and fried brown in 3 tsps. olive oil
(You may add any other vegetables you like, including: garbanzo beans, peas, or dry beans, and lentils.)
2 handfuls of your favorite macaroni or vermicelli
(You may make your own chicken or beef stock or take the easy way and use canned chicken or beef broth. My Mama would hit me with the ugly stick to hear this.)

To two large cans of chicken broth, add one can water, salt and pepper, and all the raw vegetable except potatoes. If you use canned vegetables, add them at the same time as potatoes.

Bring to a boil, turn down heat, and let simmer until the vegetables are very tender.

Dice and fry garlic in olive oil until brown, then add to soup with potatoes and canned vegetables. Let simmer until the potatoes are tender (about 15 minutes). Add salt and pepper to taste. Add vermicelli and let simmer until pasta is done.

This makes a large pot of soup, but it tastes even better the next day. If you use defatted chicken broth, it will fit almost any diet. Its good and a meal in itself with French bread!

Beef Tongue Basquaise

1 large beef tongue
1 large bell pepper
1 large pimiento
1 onion (any kind, but I like yellow onions)
1 can Ortega green chilies
1½ pounds of fresh mushrooms
3 cloves garlic
2 cans consommé soup
1 can tomato sauce (optional)

Wash tongue well, cover with water, and boil gently for about 3 hours (Add about a tablespoon of salt to the water). Peel off the skin and cut the glands under the tongue off. Let tongue cool and cut into slices.

In a seasoned Dutch oven cook peppers, onions, garlic, and mushrooms until all the vegetables are tender. Chop up the chilies and add to vegetable mixture, cooking for about 10 minutes over low heat, add the soup and sliced meat (You may add tomato sauce at this time). Cook on low heat for about half an hour. You can add salt, black pepper, and a good dash of cayenne at this time.

Just before serving, mix 2 tablespoons of corn starch in 1 cup of cold water, then add this mixture to the meat stew to thicken.

Serve immediately with plenty of French bread!

"Chilindron"

3 lbs. lamb meat
1 large onion
4 cloves garlic
6 large potatoes
salt and pepper to taste

Cut meat into large chunks and brown in Dutch oven (Lean Meat). Pour off excess fat from browned meat, then add cut up onion and garlic. Add salt and pepper and cook until onions are glossy

Cut potatoes into large chunks, salt and pepper them and add to Dutch oven. Add about 1 cup water. Let the whole mixture steam for a few minutes.

Put into 350 degree, pre-heated oven after giving the mixture a good top-to bottom- stir. Let it cook in oven for about one and a half hours. Again plenty of French bread and red wine!

"Esne Opilla" Flan

1½ quarts of milk
6 eggs
1 tablespoon sugar
⅛ teaspoon salt
1½ cups sugar (caramelized)

Put cups of sugar in custard pan on low heat. Let the sugar melt and brown, tilting the pan until all the sugar is melted and brown.

In a large bowl, beat the rest of the ingredients until they are frothy. Pour carefully into the caramelized sugar in the custard pan.

Set pan carefully in a skillet of water that comes halfway up the side of the custard pan.

Bake the pan in the skillet at 350 degrees for about an hour, or until the top is browning and a toothpick inserted into middle comes out clean. Cool and invert onto a deep plate

Leg of Lamb

1 leg of lamb
salt and pepper
4 cloves garlic

Cut slits into meaty part of leg and insert slices of garlic into slits until you use all the garlic.

Salt and pepper leg of lamb with about 1 tablespoon salt and a teaspoon of black pepper (more or less). Remember, these are hit and miss because I have had to guess at the amounts.

Put in a baking dish, cover with foil, and bake at 350 degrees or so for about 3 hours. (You can also put the whole thing into a brown bag, oh I can see mama frowning). This trick cuts baking time by at least an hour and the meat is still juicy!

Poulet Basquaise (Basque Chicken)

1 cut up chicken
3 slices bacon
1 red bell pepper
1 green bell pepper
2 cloves garlic
1 can stewed tomatoes
½ lb thinly sliced ham
1 lb mushrooms.

Fry bacon until crispy, remove from fry pan, and brown seasoned chicken until no longer pink.

Cook peppers, garlic and ham in same pan you cooked the bacon and chicken. Pour off excess drippings and add tomatoes and mushrooms.

Put chicken in baking pan, add tomatoes and vegetables, crumble cooked bacon over the top, cover with foil, and cook about 1 hour at 325-350 oven.

Bacalau (Salsa Churia) Codfish (White Sauce)

Prepare cod fillets by soaking in cold water for at least 2 days and nights, changing water frequently (this is if you use dry salt cod, otherwise use fresh fillets of cod).

Roll fillets in beaten egg then flour and quickly fry in olive oil until browned and flaky.

Fry 1½ tablespoons diced onion and two cloves of garlic then stir in 4 tablespoons flour but don't let it get brown. Add 2 cups milk, stiring in the flour mixture.

Cook until thick, about 7 or 8 minutes, then add salt and pepper to taste. Strain sauce, add 1 teaspoon of finely chopped fresh parsley, then pour over cod fillets. Serve while hot.

Bacalau Salsa Gorria Cod In Red Sauce

Prepare cod fillets in the same manner as for those in previous white sauce recipe (Bacalau Codfish, page 150). Fry quickly in olive oil and set aside. (Again, season fillets if you use fresh fish)

1 onion
1 bell pepper
1 red pepper
2 cloves garlic
½ cup white wine
1 can diced tomatoes
1 tsp. sugar
salt and pepper to taste

Fry onions, peppers, and garlic in oil until very soft. Then add tomatoes, wine, and sugar.

Cook until slightly thickened. Put fried fillets in baking pan, put a spoonful of the tomato pepper mixture on each fillet then add another layer of fish and another layer of sauce until the pan is full and all the ingredients have been used.

Cover with foil and bake at 325 degrees for about 45 minutes.

Sheepherder Potatoes

Cook four slices of bacon in a large Dutch oven then add 1 large sliced onion and 3 or 4 cloves of garlic.

Pour off any excess grease (you don't usually have any to spare). Add 6 or 8 large peeled potatoes, and salt and pepper to taste.

Optional: You may add 1 chopped bell pepper when you add potatoes.
Cook over low heat in covered Dutch oven. Stir quite often as potatoes sometimes stick! (You may add ½ cup water or broth if this occurs).

If you are lucky enough to have any leftovers, put them into a fry pan and heat. Add 2 or 3 beaten eggs (seasoned) and pour over heated potatoes. Cook until eggs are no longer runny. These are wonderful for an early morning breakfast!

Moskorr Salda/Garlic Soup

4 cloves diced garlic
2 tablespoons olive oil
pinch of salt and pepper
4 cups water
½ tsp. cayenne pepper (more if you like it spicy)
2 cups dried cubed bread
4 eggs

Fry garlic in oil until golden brown, add water, seasonings, and bread cubes.

Wait until bread is sopped (you may need more water), then drop whole eggs on top of the soup.

Lower the heat, cover, and let it steam until the eggs are well poached.

Serve hot, it's been known to cure hangovers!

Basque Beans

1 package pinto beans
3 slices bacon or ham
2–3 sliced chorizos
1 diced onion
4 cloves diced garlic
Salt and pepper to taste
1 can tomato sauce

Cook beans as directed on package.

Cook all other ingredients, except tomato sauce, remove most of the excess grease.

In Dutch oven combine all ingredients with beans, which you have drained (retain about 2 cups of cooking liquid). Cook slowly, adding tomato sauce at this time. It will be slightly thickened and you may add more liquid. Be sure to use low heat so the beans don't burn.

Sheepherder Sandwich

1 long French bread loaf
1 ½ tablespoons olive oil
½ onion, thinly sliced
3 cloves garlic (diced)
6 eggs
2 tablespoons milk or cream
dash of salt, pepper, and cayenne to taste
1 bell pepper
½ teaspoon dried parsley

Slice bread length wise, butter lightly, and set aside.

Sauté onion, pepper, and garlic in olive oil in a large frying pan. Add seasonings and dried parsley when onions are browning.

Beat 6 eggs and milk together, add seasonings (a little), pour over onion-pepper mix, and let omelet cook. Turn over just once and cook until egg is well cooked. Thickly spread inside the sliced loaf of breadand wrap in foil until you are ready to eat.

You may wish to put a big slice of fried ham or a couple of cooked chorizos on top of the omelet before wrapping in foil.

This will feed about three people, so you may wish to adjust for less.

Kauzerac / French Doughnuts

1 cup water
¼ teaspoon salt
½ cup Crisco shortening
¼ teaspoon sugar
1 cup flour
4 eggs
Oil for frying

Bring water, salt, Crisco, and sugar to a brisk boil, add flour all at once, and stir until it forms a ball and follows spoon around the pan.

Let cool a minute, then add eggs one at a time until the egg is absorbed.

In the meantime, heat Crisco or oil to very high heat in a deep fryer or deep pan.

Drop batter by spoonful's into hot cooking oil. The doughnuts will turn themselves; watch carefully because they cook very quickly. Remove with slotted spoon and roll quickly in a mixture of 1 cup sugar and 1½ tsps. cinnamon. Serve warm.

Lapina / Rabbit

1 cut up rabbit
2 big diced carrots
1 large onion
2 cloves diced garlic
2 cups white wine
½ cup water or broth
1½ tablespoons olive oil (for sauté)
Salt and pepper
1 cup flour for coating meat
1 cup olive oil for frying meat (discard after frying)

Season rabbit pieces and roll in flour. Fry meat in 1 cup olive oil and discard remaining flour and oil.

Sauté carrots, onion, garlic in sauté oil, then add fried rabbit, wine, and broth. Cover in Dutch oven or a pan with tight fitting lid. Simmer for approximately 1½ hours over low heat, or put in a hot oven at 350 degrees.

Bring on the French bread and enjoy!

Basque Potato Salad

6 medium red potatoes
4 hard boiled eggs
1 large purple onion (thinly sliced)
Salt and pepper to taste
¼ cup olive oil
½ cup wine vinegar

Boil potatoes gently for about 15 to 20 minutes or until a knife inserted tells you the potato is done (don't cook until they fall apart). Let cool, peel and slice into rounds.
Peel eggs and also slice into rounds.

Thinly slice onion, add salt, pepper olive oil and vinegar.

Mix thoroughly and serve warm if you like, or let it cool. It will taste good the next day.

You may add more oil and vinegar if you like it tart!

Soldier Creek, Ruby Mountains

GLOSSARY

Editors Note: The author uses Basque terms throughout this book. They are in the dialect that she learned as a child. In this glossary they are given with modern Batua Basque equivalents and English definitions.

Aita. Father

Aita Haundia – *aita handia.* Literally, "big father"; used to refer to her uncle the priest

Astelehena azte gusis – *Astelehena aste guziz.* There is a Monday every week.

Basquaise. Basque adjective in French

bertziak – *bertsoak.* Verses created by a bertsolari, an improvised Basque verse singer

bertzolaria – *bertsolari.* Verse improviser

chaharrac – *zaharrak.* Old

chilindron – *txilindron.* Stew

esne opilla. Flan

familiar – *familia.* Family

gatu beltza – *katu beltza.* Black cat

ikhusten ezdien begiak ezdu eguiten bate nigarric – *Ikusten ez duten begiak, ez dute bat ere negarrik egiten.* Eyes that don't see, don't cry

koska – *koska.* Bite

laminak – *laminak.* Fairies in Basque mythology

latzaharria – *latzharria.* Rough stone used as a scrub board to wash clothes

matanza – *txerri hiltzea* or *txerri boda.* Term used to refer to the time the pigs are butchered

moina. *Moño* (Spanish) or a hair bun

murcillas. *Morcilla* (Spanish), *tripota.* Blood sausage

mus. Basque card game

ogia. Wheat

otto – *oseba/izeba.* Term used in Iparralde for uncle

pasaya saria. Term used to refer of payment of passage to America for a sibling

sorgiñas – *sorginak.* Witches

talo – *taloa.* Bread made of corn meal resembling a Mexican tortilla

THE AUTHOR

Joan (Paris) Errea was born in Ely, Nevada and was raised in the sheep camp during her early years, until her father Arnaud Paris purchased a cattle ranch in White Pine County. He later sold his bands of sheep in Elko and White Pine County and purchased the Miller Ranch, in Pleasant Valley near Winnemucca, from the Stewart-Polkinghorne holdings.

She attended her first school years on the ranch with her four brothers, Arnaud, Mike, John and Pete, then moved to Winnemucca to attend upper grades and high school in the town. She married Louis Errea from Baigorri, France, who came to the states to herd sheep.

The couple have two children, son Mike and daughter Lianne. Mike, not yet married, pursues a career with the Nevada State Highway Department, and

Lianne is married to local attorney John Iroz, whose parents also came from the "old country." The Iroz's have their own law office where they work together and are the proud parents of Martin, who is the apple of Grandma's (Amatchi's) eye. The author retired from her employment as a technician in the Department of Motor Vehicles early in 1997.

Her plans now include completing a lifelong dream of creating a children's book and spending time with her own precious grandson, Martin, who already shows a great love of "stories" and books and will drop whatever he is doing for a story.

The author's first book, *A Man Called Aita,* was written in verse in honor of her father who was a poet and singer. Aita, meaning Daddy, is the story of Arnaud Paris who came a Basque immigrant from Lasa, France to herd sheep, first in Wyoming and then in Nevada, where he soon purchased his own herds of sheep and cattle. It was in Nevada that he met and married Marie Jeanne Goyhenetche who had come to Nevada to cook at a Basque Hotel in Eureka (She was my mama Marie).

www.ingramcontent.com/pod-product-compliance
Lightning Source LLC
LaVergne TN
LVHW090948080826
845145LV00003B/927

* 9 7 8 1 9 3 5 7 0 9 3 9 8 *